Cooking Italian

DESSERTS

THUNDER BAY
P·R·E·S·S

Editorial Director: Cristina Cappa Legora
Editorial Coordinator: Valeria Camaschella
Translation: Studio Traduzioni Vecchia, Milan
North American Edition
Managing Editor: JoAnn Padgett
Associate Editor: Elizabeth McNulty

Table of Contents

First published in the United States by

Thunder Bay Press
5880 Oberlin Drive, Suite 400
San Diego, CA 92121-4794
1-800-284-3580
http://www.advmkt.com

ISBN 1-57145-198-6

Library of Congress Cataloging-in-Publication Data available upon request

Printed in Singapore

1 2 3 4 5 99 00 01 02 03

Introduction

Cooking is a necessity and a pleasure. Or rather, necessity is transformed into pleasure. Today, we like to try out new ingredients whenever we can, inventing variations on traditional dishes, and experimenting with unusual types of cooking procedures.

This new series of books was designed to make cooking a pleasant pastime, with recipes based on our tradition that nevertheless often contain a little something extra, a flash of imagination, an exotic variation that makes the dish more appetizing and impressive.

The books you'll peruse will include a number of tools to help you achieve the best possible results without making mistakes or wasting time. First of all, look at the summary in each section, which will give you an immediate overview of the dishes included. The color illustrations will help you quickly choose the recipe you like best.

The recipes themselves are designed to be as practical as possible. The ingredients are clearly listed to the side, followed by the equipment necessary and a practical chart that summarizes everything you need to know right away, before you begin cooking: the degree of difficulty, preparation and cooking time, cooking method, how long the dish will keep, and so on. The description of the recipes is also extremely clear and detailed, and is divided into sections that cover each separate stage of the recipe.

Another important feature is the suggestion of an appropriate wine to be served with the dish. (These are just suggestions because we all know that wines are a matter of personal taste.) As this is a light dessert cookbook, treat these as recipes for desserts: serve pleasant white wines or rosés, sweet or raisin wines, or any kind of red dessert wine. To make it easier for you, we have always selected wines with appellation contrôlée, with the official caption. Of course, we also provide the best temperature for serving each individual wine.

In addition, there are always practical, useful suggestions on the recipe itself (for example, whether you can change any ingredients, how to multiply a given dish), or related to preparation.

Finally, we include a "special note" for each preparation—some extra information on an ingredient in the recipe that may be historical, scientific, dietetic and so forth—that further enriches the descriptions.

This book is devoted to light DESSERTS, and the recipes are broken down into Cakes, Tortes and Pies, Spoon Desserts, and Fruit Salad and More. We offer you many new ways to complete a meal in an original, tasty and healthful way.

Recipe Index

Cakes, Tortes and Pies

Blackberry Timbale

INGREDIENTS
serves 4

For the puff pastry
1 2/3 cups – 200 g WHITE FLOUR
1 1/8 cups – 100 g SUGAR
1 tablespoon GRATED LEMON ZEST
1 pinch SALT
3 EGG YOLKS
1/2 cup – 100 g BUTTER plus a walnut–sized piece for the quiche pan

For the filling
1 lb. – 400 g BLACKBERRIES
3 tablespoons full – 80 g SUGAR
1 tablespoon GRATED LEMON ZEST
1 pinch CINNAMON
1 pinch NUTMEG

EQUIPMENT
2 mixing bowls, a quiche dish, a serving dish

Difficulty	**AVERAGE**
Preparation Time	**30 MIN. + 30 MIN.**
Cooking Time	**50 MIN.**
Method of cooking	**OVEN**
Microwave	**YES**
Freezing	**YES**
Keeping Time	**3 DAYS**

SPECIAL NOTE
Blackberries grow wild in thorny bushes, which thrive in various areas of the world, even in mountains as high as 3,000 feet.

RECOMMENDED WINES
Moscato d'Asti (Piedmont): aged red wine served at 46°F / 8°C
Malvasia di Cagliari (Sardinia): aged red wine served at 46°F / 8°C

1 Prepare the puff pastry. Sift the flour and sugar together, mound them on a rolling board and in the center place the grated lemon zest, the salt, the egg yolks and the previously softened and chopped butter. Blend the ingredients well and quickly make a dough.

2 When you have a smooth, uniform dough, shape it into a loaf, cover with a kitchen towel and let it rest for a half hour in a cool place.

3 In the meantime, prepare the filling. Trim and wash the blackberries, drain well and place in a mixing bowl. Add the sugar, lemon zest, a pinch of cinnamon and a pinch of nutmeg, and mix gently.

4 Take out the dough and roll it out, not too thinly. Butter the quiche dish, line it with two thirds of the puff pastry and fill with the blackberry mixture. Cut a disk from the remaining dough, cover the torte with this, sealing the edges well, and place in a preheated 400°F oven for about 50 minutes. Serve cold, and decorate with more blackberries if you like.

PRACTICAL SUGGESTIONS
If you're in a hurry, you can buy ready–made puff pastry. You can also use other berries, such as blueberries, alpine strawberries, or raspberries.

Fig and Peach Torte

Recommended Wines
Riviera Ligure di Ponente Pigato (Liguria):
dry white wine served at 50°F / 10°C
Trebbiano di Romagna (Emilia Romagna):
dry white wine served at 50°F / 10°C

1 Remove the stems from the figs, completely removing the portion that contains the milky substance, then wash and dry. Place three quarters of the butter in a frying pan and heat. As soon as it becomes foamy, add the figs and fry 6–8 minutes, turning often to brown them well on all sides. When they are done, remove them from the pan with a slotted spoon, being careful not to break them, and place on absorbent paper towels to remove any excess grease.

2 Wash and peel the peaches, remove the pit and slice. Fry in the same seasoning as for the figs, turning often, for 7–8 minutes, until they lose all their moisture, then place them and the seasoning in a large mixing bowl and cool.

3 Add the crumbled cookies and macaroon, the beaten egg and yolk, and the sugar to the peaches and mix well, moistening with the rum. Brush a baking pan with the remaining butter, flour it and pour in the mixture. Using the back of a spoon, make hollows in which you place the figs. Place the pan in a preheated 210°F oven for about 3 hours, as the dessert must dry slowly. When done, remove from the oven, cool and serve in the baking dish.

Practical Suggestions
To peel the peaches without difficulty, just immerse them for a few moments in a skillet of boiling water.

INGREDIENTS
serves 4

8 ripe but firm FIGS
1/4 cup – 40 g BUTTER
3 WHITE PEACHES
2 oz. – 40 g PLAIN COOKIES, crumbled
1 MACAROON
1 EGG
1 EGG YOLK
1 1/8 cups – 100 g SUGAR
2 tablespoons RUM
WHITE FLOUR as necessary

EQUIPMENT
a frying pan
a slotted spoon
absorbent paper towels
a mixing bowl
a baking pan

Difficulty	**AVERAGE**
Preparation Time	**30 MIN.**
Cooking Time	**3 HOURS + 15 MIN.**
Method of cooking	**STOVETOP AND OVEN**
Microwave	**NO**
Freezing	**NO**
Keeping Time	**3 DAYS**

SPECIAL NOTE
Fig trees grow especially well where olives and citrus thrive. In Italy, two domestic and wild species *(caprifico)* are particularly common.

Pineapple Puff Pastry Cake

INGREDIENTS

serves 6

1/2 lb. – 200 g READY-MADE PUFF PASTRY
half a PINEAPPLE
3 oz. – 80 g APRICOT GELATIN
2 CANDIED CHERRIES

EQUIPMENT

a rolling pin
a baking sheet
a small saucepan
a flat brush
a serving dish

Difficulty	AVERAGE
Preparation Time	25 MIN.
Cooking Time	25 MIN.
Method of cooking	STOVETOP AND OVEN
Microwave	YES
Freezing	YES
Keeping Time	3 DAYS

SPECIAL NOTE

Pineapple is the fruit of a tropical plant in the Bromeliaceae family; a single pineapple may weigh as much as 11 pounds. Originally from Brazil or Paraguay, pineapples reached Europe in the 16th century.

RECOMMENDED WINES

Gioia del Colle Aleatico dolce (Puglia): aged red wine served at 50°F / 10°C
Albana di Romagna passito (Emilia Romagna): liqueur–like wine or dry raisin wine served at 50°F / 10°C

1 Using a rolling pin, roll the dough out thinly. Cut out a square about 10 inches in size and place it on a lightly moistened baking sheet. Using a knife, cut 4 strips of pastry a little under a half an inch – 1 centimeter wide along the edges of the square.

2 Lightly brush the edges of the remaining square with water, place the cut strips on it, pressing along the edges with a fork, and roll the ends up into a spiral. Poke holes in the surface of the pastry with a fork. Place the sheet in a preheated 400°F oven and bake 20 minutes, then remove the sheet from the oven and cool the pastry completely. In the meantime, peel the pineapple and chop it into horizontal slices about a quarter inch – half a centimeter thick. Remove the hard center portion and cut them into four pieces each.

3 Melt the apricot gelatin in a small saucepan with 2 tablespoons water, then use a flat brush to spread a thin layer on the pastry. Harmoniously arrange the pineapple pieces on the pastry, garnish with the chopped candied cherries and brush everything with the remaining apricot gelatin. Transfer to a serving dish and serve.

PRACTICAL SUGGESTIONS

You can also use canned pineapples to prepare this puff pastry dessert. Use pineapples packed in natural liquid and drain well.

Whole-Wheat Plum Tart

INGREDIENTS
serves 4

I scant cup – 100 g WHOLE-WHEAT FLOUR
I scant cup – 100 g WHITE FLOUR
I 1/3 cups – 130 g SUGAR
3 EGGS
1/4 cup – 50 g BUTTER
I GRATED LEMON ZEST
1.5 lb. – 600 g PLUMS
half a cup MARASCHINO LIQUEUR
I scant cup – 2 dl MILK

For the quiche pan
I walnut-sized chunk BUTTER
I tablespoon WHITE FLOUR

EQUIPMENT
a bowl, a rolling pin
a quiche pan, a mixing bowl
a serving dish

Difficulty	AVERAGE
Preparation Time	30 MIN. + 30 MIN.
Cooking Time	40 MIN.
Method of cooking	OVEN
Microwave	YES
Freezing	YES
Keeping Time	4 DAYS

SPECIAL NOTE
Plums are the fruit of various species of trees in the genus *Prunus.* When dried, they are called prunes. Fresh plums are used in this recipe.

RECOMMENDED WINES
Alto Adige moscato giallo (Trentino Alto Adige): liqueur–like wine or sweet raisin wine served at 46°F / 8°C
Montefalco Sagrantino passito (Umbria): liqueur–like wine or dry raisin wine served at 50°F / 10°C

1 Sift the two flours together on a rolling board with a little under half the sugar (60 grams). Place an egg, the butter and the grated lemon zest in the center, and quickly make a dough, using the tips of your fingers. Form a ball, wrap in a damp cloth and let it rest 30 minutes in the least cold area of the refrigerator.

2 In the meantime, wash the plums, remove the pits, and chop the pulp into pieces. Place in a bowl and drizzle with the Maraschino liqueur and set aside. Take out the dough and using a rolling pin, roll it out about 1/8 inch – 3 mm thick. Transfer to a buttered, floured quiche pan and poke holes in it with a fork.

3 In a mixing bowl, lightly beat the 2 eggs with the remaining sugar, add the milk and mix well. Place the plums in the cake pan and pour in the egg, sugar and milk mixture.

4 Cut thin disks from the remaining scraps of pastry and use them to decorate the surface of the tart as you like. Bake in a preheated 350°F oven for 40 minutes. When done, cool, place on a serving dish and serve.

PRACTICAL SUGGESTIONS
You can prepare this tart using prunes instead of plums, and if you want to serve it as a children's snack, you can dilute the Maraschino with a few spoonfuls of water.

Kiwi Dessert

INGREDIENTS

serves 4

6 KIWIS
2/3 cup – 3 dl MARSALA WINE
1/4 cup – 1 dl DRY WHITE WINE
6 EGG YOLKS
1 1/3 cups – 120 g SUGAR
1/3 cup – 50 g WHITE FLOUR
3 tablespoons – 1 dl CREAM
1 READY-MADE SPONGE CAKE
8–9 inches – 22 cm in diameter

EQUIPMENT

2 mixing bowls
2 bowls
a saucepan
a spring mold
a serving dish

Difficulty	AVERAGE
Preparation Time	20 MIN. + 4 HOURS
Cooking Time	5 MIN.
Method of cooking	STOVETOP
Microwave	NO
Freezing	YES
Keeping Time	2 DAYS

SPECIAL NOTE

In Italy, kiwis were once considered an exotic fruit. Today they are extremely popular at Italian tables and are widely cultivated as well. In fact, Italy now contends with New Zealand for the position of number one producer in the world.

RECOMMENDED WINES

Bianco di Valdinievole Vin Santo (Tuscany): liqueur–like wine or dry raisin wine served at 50°F / 10°C

Collio Goriziano Picolit (Friuli–Venezia Giulia): liqueur–like wine or dry raisin wine served at 50°F / 10°C

1 Peel the kiwis and chop into rather thin slices. Place in a mixing bowl, add the marsala and the white wine, and let them soak for about an hour. Then drain and set aside.

2 Beat the egg yolks and sugar with a spoon in a bowl until they have become clear and foamy. Add the flour and the liquid the kiwis soaked in, and carefully mix. Pour the mixture in a saucepan, turn on the heat, bring to a boil and cook the custard for 3–4 minutes. Remove from the heat, pour into a bowl and cool, stirring occasionally. When the custard is completely cooled, gently add the cream, which you have whipped in a separate bowl.

3 Using a sharp knife, cut the sponge cake into 3 horizontal layers. Place one layer in the spring mold, add a bit of the prepared custard and spread uniformly. Add a layer of kiwis, then another layer of sponge cake, a layer of custard and one of kiwis. End with the last layer of sponge cake, cover with the remaining custard and garnish with the remaining slices of kiwi. Refrigerate the dessert for 3 hours. When ready to serve, remove from the mold, place on a serving dish and serve.

PRACTICAL SUGGESTIONS

You can tell if a kiwi is ripe by holding it between your thumb and forefinger and squeezing lightly. It should be slightly soft but firm. To quickly ripen green fruit, leave it in a basket with an apple, at room temperature.

Blueberry Torte

INGREDIENTS
serves 6–8

For the dough
6 tablespoons MILK, 3 tablespoons SUGAR
1/2 cup – 100 g BUTTER, 1/2 oz. BAKER'S YEAST, 2 1/2 cups – 300 g WHITE FLOUR
pinch of SALT, 2 EGGS

For the filling
3/4 lb. – 300 g BLUEBERRIES
1 1/8 cups – 100 g SUGAR

To garnish
1.5 oz. – 30 g BLUEBERRIES
1 teaspoon APRICOT GELATIN, 1 tablespoon POWDERED SUGAR, a few MINT leaves

EQUIPMENT
a round quiche pan about
10 inches – 24–26 cm in diameter
2 saucepans, 2 small bowls, a mixing bowl

Difficulty	**AVERAGE**
Preparation Time	**35 MIN. + 13 HOURS**
Cooking Time	**1 HOUR + 10 MIN.**
Method of cooking	**STOVETOP AND OVEN**
Microwave	**YES**
Freezing	**NO**
Keeping Time	**3 DAYS**

SPECIAL NOTE
Blueberries are a member of the heath family. About 90% of the world's blueberries are grown in North America.

RECOMMENDED WINES
Oltrepò Pavese moscato liquoroso (Lombardy): liqueur–like wine or dry raisin wine served at 50°F / 10°C
Gambellara Vin Santo (Veneto): liqueur–like wine or dry raisin wine served at 50°F / 10°C

1 Heat the milk, sugar and butter to lukewarm in a saucepan, then add the yeast, dissolved in 2 tablespoons lukewarm water. Sift the flour and salt together. Add the eggs and prepared mixture, and knead the dough for 20 minutes, lifting it and slapping it down occasionally. Cover it with a cloth and allow it to rise in a warm place for about 30 minutes. Then knead it again for a few moments to stop it from rising. Place it in the mixing bowl again, cover it with a damp cloth and place it in the warmest part of the refrigerator for 12 hours. Then remove it from the bowl and knead it again a little on the cutting board.

2 Wash the blueberries, place them in a saucepan with the sugar, place over the heat and bring to a boil. Cook for 10–15 minutes, stirring often. Roll out half the dough and place it in a buttered, floured quiche pan, pour the blueberry mixture in the center and spread it, leaving a half inch – 1 cm border. Place the remaining dough over it and press down the edges to seal. Let it rise in a warm place for 30–40 minutes, then bake in a preheated 350°F oven for 45 minutes. Cool. Prepare the garnish. Wash the garnish blueberries, drain, dry and place in a small bowl. Heat the gelatin with 1 tablespoon water, pour over the blueberries and mix. Sprinkle with powdered sugar and place the blueberries in the center, surrounded by mint leaves.

PRACTICAL SUGGESTIONS
The success of this dessert depends on the dough. It has been kneaded enough when it no longer sticks to the mixing bowl or your hands and becomes smooth, soft and elastic.

Custard and Sour Cherry Torte

INGREDIENTS
serves 6–8

For the dough
2 cups – 250 g WHITE FLOUR
1 teaspoon VANILLA
3/4 cup – 120 g BUTTER
3/4 cup – 70 g SUGAR, 1 EGG YOLK
grated zest of half a LEMON
1 oz. – 20 g crumbled DRY COOKIES

For the custard
2 cups – 80 g WHOLE MILK
zest of one LEMON, 4 EGG YOLKS
1 teaspoon VANILLA, 1 cup – 80 g SUGAR
1/4 cup – 40 g WHITE FLOUR
3/4 lb. – 300 g SOUR CHERRIES IN SYRUP

EQUIPMENT
a skillet, a rolling pin, a mixing bowl
a small saucepan, a quiche pan, a serving dish

Difficulty	**AVERAGE**
Preparation Time	**30 MIN. + 30 MIN.**
Cooking Time	**1 HOUR 15 MIN.**
Method of cooking	**STOVETOP AND OVEN**
Microwave	**NO**
Freezing	**NO**
Keeping Time	**3 DAYS**

SPECIAL NOTE
The sour cherry is a tarter version of the black cherry. The various cultivars in Italy have different names, such as *marena, visciola* and *marasca,* from which the famous Maraschino liqueur is made.

RECOMMENDED WINES
Trentino Moscato Rosa (Trentino Alto Adige): liqueur–like wine or sweet raisin wine served at 50°F / 10°C
Bianco di Scandiano spumante (Emilia–Romagna): aged red wine served at 46°F / 8°C

1 Sift the flour, mound onto the rolling board, and add the vanilla, the chopped butter, the sugar, the egg yolk and the lemon zest. Work rapidly to form a ball, wrap in a cloth, place in the warmest part of the refrigerator and let it rest for a half hour.

2 In the meantime, prepare the custard. Boil the milk in a skillet with the lemon zest; mix the egg yolks, vanilla and sugar in a mixing bowl, add the sifted flour, mix and gradually add the hot milk, stirring often to prevent it from forming lumps. Transfer the mixture to a small saucepan and bring to a boil. Cook 8 minutes, stirring often, then let it cool.

3 Roll out the dough and line the buttered, floured pan with it. Set aside the scraps of dough. Poke holes in it with a fork, sprinkle with the cookies, pour half the custard on one layer, and add a layer of cherries (setting 2 tablespoons aside). Pour the remaining custard over it and smooth the surface. Roll out the scraps of dough, cut out strips a little less than an inch – 2 centimeters wide, and arrange them crosswise on the custard in a grid pattern. In each space, place one of the cherries you set aside. Bake at 350°F for one hour. When done, remove and let the torte sit before turning it out of the pan. Place it on a serving dish and serve cold.

PRACTICAL SUGGESTIONS
If you're in a hurry, you can prepare the dough the day before. Wrap in aluminum foil and keep it in the refrigerator until use.

Peach and Almond Jam Tart

INGREDIENTS
serves 6

For the dough
1 1/3 cups – 160 g WHITE FLOUR
1/2 cup – 50 g SUGAR
1/3 cup – 80 g BUTTER

For the custard
2 cups – half a liter MILK
1 VANILLA bean
3 EGG YOLKS
1 1/2 cups – 130 g SUGAR
2 oz. – 50 g POTATO (or corn) STARCH

For the garnish
1 large can PEACHES IN SYRUP
4 oz. – 100 g slivered ALMONDS

EQUIPMENT
2 skillets, a mixing bowl, a rolling pin
a quiche pan, aluminum foil
dry beans, a serving dish

Difficulty	AVERAGE
Preparation Time	30 MIN. +1 HOUR
Cooking Time	30 MIN.
Method of cooking	STOVETOP AND OVEN
Microwave	NO
Freezing	NO
Keeping Time	3 DAYS

SPECIAL NOTE
Yellow peaches are not as early or as fragrant, but because they are larger, colorful and easy to conserve, they are more commonly cultivated.

RECOMMENDED WINES
Colli Orientali del Friuli Ramandolo (Friuli Venezia Giulia): aged red wine served at 50°F / 10°C
Vin Santo del Chianti Classico (Tuscany): liqueur-like wine or dry raisin wine served at 50°F / 10°C

1 Mound the flour on the rolling board, add the sugar and butter, softened and chopped into pieces, and quickly make a uniform dough. Form it into a ball, wrap it in a kitchen cloth and let it sit in a cool place for an hour.

2 In the meantime, bring the milk to boil in a skillet with the vanilla bean, cut in half lengthwise, then drizzle it into the egg yolks (which you have beaten well in a mixing bowl with the sugar and potato starch). Pour the mixture into another skillet, and continuing to mix with a wooden spoon, allow the custard to thicken.

3 Take out the dough and roll it out not too thinly. Place it in a buttered cake pan, covering the sides as well. Poke holes in the dough with a fork, cover it with aluminum foil and place the dry beans on it. Bake in a preheated 350° oven about 20 minutes.

4 When done, turn out the tart, remove the beans and aluminum foil, cool and turn out onto a serving dish. Pour the custard into the puff pastry, then add the peaches, well-drained from their liquid, and sprinkle everything with slivered almonds.

PRACTICAL SUGGESTIONS
You can use four fresh peaches for this tart instead of canned peaches in syrup. To peel them easily, remember to toss them into boiling water for a few seconds, drain, and immediately run under cold water.

Grape and Apple Tart

Recommended Wines
Oltrepò Pavese Moscato (Lombardy): aged red wine served at 50°F / 10°C
Malvasia di Bosa (Sardinia): aged red wine served at 50°F / 10°C

1 Wash and peel the apples, core them with a corer or small knife and cut them into rounds about a quarter inch – half a centimeter thick. Pick the grapes from the bunch, wash and dry them. Crush the macaroons into a powder and mix them with the cocoa.

2 Butter a spring mold and sprinkle with the crushed cookies. Make a layer of apples on the bottom and place a grape in the center of each apple round. Sprinkle the apple layer with a pinch of cinnamon and part of the macaroon and cocoa mixture. Make two more layers, alternating the apple rounds with the macaroon mixture.

3 Mix the egg yolks with the sugar in a mixing bowl, add the flour mixed with the baking powder, the cream and the egg whites, beaten to stiff peaks. Pour the mixture on the apples, add a few dots of butter and bake in a preheated 350°F oven for 45 minutes.

4 When the torte is ready, allow it to cool, then turn it out upside down, place in a serving dish and sprinkle with powdered sugar.

Practical Suggestions
You can also prepare this "upside down cake" by first caramelizing the layer of apples on the bottom of the pan with butter and sugar, then proceeding as indicated in the recipe.

INGREDIENTS
serves 4

2.2 lb. – 1 kg TART APPLES
1 bunch GREEN GRAPES
6 MACAROONS
1 tablespoon SWEET COCOA
1/8 cup – 30 g BUTTER
2 tablespoons DRY PLAIN COOKIES, grated
1 pinch CINNAMON
2 EGGS
4 tablespoons SUGAR
1 scant cup – 100 g FLOUR
1 tablespoon BAKING POWDER
3 tablespoons CREAM
1/8 cup – 30 g POWDERED SUGAR

EQUIPMENT
a mixing bowl, a spring mold
a serving dish

Difficulty	**AVERAGE**
Preparation Time	**30 MIN.**
Cooking Time	**40 MIN.**
Method of cooking	**OVEN**
Microwave	**YES**
Freezing	**NO**
Keeping Time	**3 DAYS**

SPECIAL NOTE
There are over 250 varieties of apples, all excellent eaten raw. Wash them well and eat with the skin, which is rich in vitamins and fiber. For cooking, use firm apples, such as Granny Smiths.

Lemon Meringue Pie

INGREDIENTS
serves 6–8

For the dough
2 cups – 250 g WHITE FLOUR
1/3 cup – 125 g MELTED BUTTER
1 pinch SALT

For the custard
3 EGGS
4 1/2 tablespoons SUGAR
2 tablespoons CORNSTARCH
2 cups – half a liter MILK
2 LEMONS
2 tablespoons POWDERED SUGAR

EQUIPMENT
1 spring mold, a skillet
aluminum foil, a handful of dry beans
a serving dish

Difficulty	AVERAGE
Preparation Time	20 MIN. + 1 HOUR
Cooking Time	50 MIN.
Method of cooking	STOVETOP AND OVEN
Microwave	YES
Freezing	NO
Keeping Time	2 DAYS

SPECIAL NOTE
After oranges, lemons are the most widely cultivated citrus fruits in Italy. The orange tree, a native of East Asia, was introduced to the Mediterranean area by the Arabs around the year 1000.

Recommended Wines

Cinque Terre Sciacchetrà (Liguria): liqueur–like wine or dry raisin wine served at 50°F / 10°C

Gioia del Colle Aleatico liquoroso dolce (Puglia): liqueur–like wine or dry raisin wine served at 50°F / 10°C

1 Prepare the dough. Blend the flour with the butter, salt and 4 tablespoons cold water, form a ball, wrap in a cloth and let it sit in the refrigerator for an hour. Roll into a thin layer and line the buttered, floured spring mold with it. Poke holes in the bottom with a fork, cover with aluminum foil and fill with dry beans. Bake in a preheated 350°F oven for 20 minutes.

2 In the meantime, prepare the custard. Beat the egg yolks with the sugar and cornstarch, dilute the mixture slowly with cold milk, and stirring constantly with a wooden spoon, bring everything to a slow boil. Remove from the heat and add the lemon juice (pouring it in through a strainer) and a pinch of grated zest, mixing well.

3 When the pie is ready, remove the aluminum foil and beans and pour the custard over it. Smooth the surface well, then cover with the egg whites beaten to stiff peaks, and sprinkle with sifted powdered sugar. Place the pie in the oven again for 10 minutes and lightly brown the meringue under the broiler. Remove from the oven and cool the pie, then place on a serving dish and serve.

Practical Suggestions

It's best to squeeze the lemon (which should be organic) by hand and avoid using electric or manual squeezers, to prevent the pulp from being compressed against the white rind and taking on a bitter taste.

Semifreddo with Strawberries

INGREDIENTS

serves 6–8

2.2 lb. – 1 kg STRAWBERRIES
1 small glass STRAWBERRY BRANDY
2 1/3 cups – 250 g SUGAR
4 EGG WHITES, SALT to taste
3/4 lb. – 300 g WHIPPED CREAM
1 READY–MADE SPONGE CAKE
about 10–11 inches – 26 cm in diameter
1 teaspoon RUM

For the garnish

1 carton ALPINE STRAWBERRIES
1/4 lb. – 100 g WHIPPED CREAM
a few leaves FRESH MINT

EQUIPMENT

a mixing bowl, a blender, a skillet
a whip, aluminum foil, plastic wrap
a spring mold, a serving dish

Difficulty	**AVERAGE**
Preparation Time	**40 MIN. + 5 HOURS**
Cooking Time	**10 MIN.**
Method of cooking	**STOVETOP**
Microwave	**NO**
Freezing	**YES**
Keeping Time	**2 DAYS**

SPECIAL NOTE

Alpine strawberries are easy to grow anywhere in your garden. Just plant them in regular rows to create an area of dark green that will be dotted with spots of red from May to August.

RECOMMENDED WINES

Vernaccia di Serrapetrona (Marche): liqueur–like wine or dry raisin wine served at 50°F / 10°C

Moscato di Siracusa (Sicily): liqueur–like wine or sweet raisin wine served at 50°F / 10°C

1 Trim and wash the strawberries, drain them well, then whip with the brandy. Place the mixture in a mixing bowl and refrigerate. Place the sugar in a skillet, add a half a cup of water and let it melt over low heat, stirring often.

2 In the meantime, beat the egg whites to stiff peaks in a mixing bowl, with a pinch of salt, slowly add the cooled sugar syrup and continue mixing until you have a foamy mixture. Add 2/3 of the strawberry puree, mixing constantly from the bottom to the top, using a whip. Finally, add the whipped cream.

3 Now line the bottom and sides of the spring mold with aluminum foil. Pour in half the prepared mixture, place the sponge cake on top, sprinkle with rum diluted with a bit of water and pour in the remaining strawberry and cream mixture.

4 Cover the dessert with plastic wrap and leave in the freezer for 5 hours. Unmold onto a serving dish, decorate with the alpine strawberries alternating with dabs of whipped cream and fresh mint leaves. Serve with the strawberry sauce you set aside, served in a sauce boat.

PRACTICAL SUGGESTIONS

Strawberries are a delicate, widely available fruit. Treat them with care: handle them as little as possible and wash them quickly with the stem to prevent them from losing their flavor.

Orange Soufflé

INGREDIENTS

serves 6

1 cup – 1/4 liter WHOLE MILK
1 VANILLA bean
1/2 cup – 65 g WHITE FLOUR
2/3 cup – 65 g SUGAR
3 EGGS
4 EGG WHITES
1 ORANGE
2 tablespoons GRAND MARNIER
1/8 cup – 25 g BUTTER

For the mold

2 tablespoons – 25 g BUTTER
1 tablespoon SUGAR

EQUIPMENT

2 saucepans, a whip, a mixing bowl
a soufflé mold

Difficulty	**ELABORATE**
Preparation Time	**30 MIN.**
Cooking Time	**50 MIN.**
Method of cooking	**STOVETOP AND OVEN**
Microwave	**NO**
Freezing	**NO**
Keeping Time	**1 DAY**

SPECIAL NOTE

One way to eliminate bad odors from the oven is to put a few orange peels on a baking sheet and turn the oven on high for fifteen minutes.

Recommended Wines

Aglianico del Vulture Spumante (Basilicata): light sweet wine served at 46°F / 8°C
Moscato di Noto naturale (Sicily): aged red wine served at 46°F / 8°C

1 Pour the milk into a saucepan, place it on the heat, add the vanilla bean and bring it slowly to a boil. Place the flour and sugar in another saucepan, add a whole egg and a yolk (setting the white aside), the grated orange rind and the Grand Marnier, and mix well with a whip to blend the ingredients.

2 Pour in the hot milk a little at a time. Remove the vanilla bean, mix well, place the saucepan over the heat and slowly bring to a boil, mixing constantly. Cook about 2 minutes, until the mixture is smooth and uniform.

3 Remove the pan from the heat and allow the mixture to cool to lukewarm. Add the butter, the remaining egg yolk (setting aside the egg white) and fold it in gently, mixing with a wooden spoon. Beat the 6 egg whites to stiff peaks in a mixing bowl and add to the mixture.

4 Pour the mixture into a buttered soufflé mold sprinkled with sugar. Bake in a preheated 350°F oven for about 40 minutes. Serve the soufflé hot, and if you like, accompany it with a Grand Marnier sauce served in a separate sauce boat.

Practical Suggestions

Grand Marnier sauce, served lukewarm in a sauce boat, enhances the orange flavor. To prepare it, dilute bitter orange marmalade with a bit of water and half a small cup Grand Marnier.

Strawberry Brick

INGREDIENTS

serves 6

2 lb. – 800 g STRAWBERRIES
3 tablespoons SUGAR
9 tablespoons ORANGE JUICE
1 oz. – 20 g SHEET GELATIN
1/4 cup – 1 dl COINTREAU
2 oz. – 40 g LADYFINGERS
1/2 cup – 2 dl WHIPPED CREAM

EQUIPMENT

2 bowls
a vegetable mill
a mixing bowl
a skillet
a square mold
vegetable paper
plastic wrap
a serving dish

Difficulty	ELABORATE
Preparation Time	30 MIN. + 4 HOURS
Cooking Time	10 MIN.
Method of cooking	STOVETOP
Microwave	NO
Freezing	YES
Keeping Time	2 DAYS

SPECIAL NOTE

Some species of strawberry grow wild in Europe, including Italy. The best known is *Fragaria vesca*, the common alpine strawberry, which includes a number of subspecies.

RECOMMENDED WINES

Brachetto d'Acqui (Piedmont): aged red wine served at 54°F / 12°C
Colli Orientali del Friuli Ramandolo (Friuli Venezia Giulia): aged red wine served at 50°F / 10°C

1 Wash the strawberries, drain and dry. Place half in a vegetable mill and place the resulting puree in a mixing bowl. Add the sugar, mix, and place the mixture in the refrigerator. Pour 2 tablespoons orange juice in a skillet, add the gelatin (which you have previously softened in a bowl of water) and heat it slightly, mixing with a wooden spoon until melted. Add the mixture to the strawberry puree and set it aside. Mix the Cointreau in a bowl with the remaining orange juice.

2 Line the mold with the vegetable paper. Make a layer of ladyfingers, brush with the orange and Cointreau syrup, pour on a layer of strawberries in gelatin and place the dessert in the refrigerator for ten minutes so it can firm. Remove from the refrigerator, make another layer of ladyfingers, brush with the syrup and make a layer of strawberries and cream about 1/2 – 1 inch – 1–2 centimeters high. Cover with some of the remaining strawberries, sliced, and pour the remaining strawberry and cream mixture on top. End with a layer of ladyfingers brushed with the syrup. Cover the dessert with plastic wrap and refrigerate 3 hours. Remove it, take off the plastic wrap and turn out onto a serving dish. Garnish with the remaining strawberries and serve.

PRACTICAL SUGGESTIONS

To prepare this dessert, you can also use ready-made sponge cake, sliced, instead of ladyfingers. You can also decorate the surface with dabs of whipped cream.

Nectarine Clafoutis

INGREDIENTS
serves 6

For the dough
1 cup – 125 g WHITE FLOUR
1/8 teaspoon VANILLA, 1/4 cup – 60 g BUTTER
scant 1 cup – 70 g SUGAR, 1 EGG YOLK
half a LEMON

For the cake pan
2 tablespoons – 20 g BUTTER
3 tablespoons – 20 g FLOUR

For the filling
4 NECTARINES, 1/2 cup – 50 g SUGAR
2 EGGS, 4 tablespoons MILK, 1 teaspoon KIRSCH
16 – 40 g ALMONDS, finely ground

For the garnish
1 tablespoon APRICOT GELATIN
1/2 tablespoon POWDERED SUGAR

EQUIPMENT
a rectangular cake pan, a mixing bowl
a small saucepan, a rolling pin, a serving dish

Difficulty	**ELABORATE**
Preparation Time	**30 MIN. + 1 HOUR**
Cooking Time	**40 MIN.**
Method of cooking	**OVEN**
Microwave	**YES**
Freezing	**YES**
Keeping Time	**3 DAYS**

SPECIAL NOTE
Nectarines have a smooth, glossy, hairless skin, with large red spots on a lighter background. They are small in size and have an excellent flavor.

RECOMMENDED WINES

Valle d'Aosta Chambave Moscato passito (Valle d'Aosta): liqueur–like wine or dry raisin wine served at 50°F / 10°C
Sant'Antimo Vin Santo (Tuscany): liqueur–like wine or dry raisin wine served at 50°F / 10°C

1 Prepare the dough. Sift the flour into a mound on a rolling board, and add the vanilla, the softened, chopped butter, the sugar, the egg yolk and the grated lemon zest. Quickly blend with your fingertips without working the dough too long. Form it into a ball, wrap in a cloth and let it sit in the warmest part of the refrigerator for at least an hour. Then take it out and use the rolling pin to roll it out to about 1/8 inch – 3 mm. Butter and flour the cake pan and place the dough in it. Repeatedly poke the bottom with a fork and pinch the edges all around.

2 Prepare the filling. Wash the nectarines, peel, cut into slices and place in the cake pan. Place the sugar, eggs, milk and kirsch in a mixing bowl, add the ground almonds and mix with a wooden spoon until the ingredients are well blended. Pour the batter over the nectarines, then bake in a preheated 350°F oven for 30–40 minutes. Remove from oven, turn the tart out onto a serving dish and cool. In the meantime, prepare the garnish. Bring the gelatin to a boil in a small saucepan with a tablespoon water, brush the edges of the dessert and sprinkle powdered sugar over it. Serve.

PRACTICAL SUGGESTIONS

If you can't find nectarines, use yellow peaches instead, provided they are large and juicy. If you make this dessert in the winter, you can use canned peaches instead.

Pear Tart

INGREDIENTS

serves 4

2 1/2 cups – 300 g WHITE FLOUR
1 1/4 cups – 130 g SUGAR
1 tablespoon BAKING POWDER
1/2 cup – 100 g BUTTER
1 EGG
1 1/2 lb. – 600 g PEARS
2 tablespoons LEMON JUICE

EQUIPMENT

a rolling pin
a bowl
a round quiche pan about
10–11 inches – 26 cm in diameter
a serving dish

Difficulty	AVERAGE
Preparation Time	20 MIN.
Cooking Time	40 MIN.
Method of cooking	OVEN
Microwave	NO
Freezing	YES
Keeping Time	3–4 DAYS

SPECIAL NOTE

The pear is an extremely ancient fruit; even in Roman times, about 40 varieties were known. Italy is still one of the largest pear producers in the world.

RECOMMENDED WINES

Colli di Parma Malvasia Spumante (Emilia–Romagna): aged red wine served at 50°F / 10°C

Nasco di Cagliari liquoroso dolce (Sardinia): liqueur–like wine or dry raisin wine served at 50°F / 10°C

1 Sift the flour onto the cutting board, add 1 cup sugar and the baking powder, make a hole in the center and add the softened, chopped butter and the egg.

2 Quickly form a dough using your fingertips. When it is well–blended, roll it out and line the buttered, lightly floured quiche pan with it. Poke holes in the dough with a fork.

3 Wash the pears, dry and peel them, remove the cores and seeds and slice thinly. Place in a bowl, drizzle with the lemon juice, and mix.

4 Arrange the pears in concentric circles on the dough in the quiche pan, and sprinkle with the remaining sugar. Bake the tart in a preheated 350°F oven for about 40 minutes. When done, remove, turn out onto a serving dish and cool completely before serving.

PRACTICAL SUGGESTIONS

All pears are quite perishable, so you should buy them a little green and leave them at room temperature, until the flesh has become slightly soft to the touch.

Chestnut Cream Roll

Recommended Wines

Spumante Moscato di Santa Maria La Versa (Lombardy): aged red wine served at 50°F / 10°C

Cannonau di Sardegna Superiore dolce (Sardinia): aged red wine served at 50°F / 10°C

1 Using the beater, beat the egg yolks with the sugar in a mixing bowl. When they are well beaten, add the vanilla and the flour and potato flour (sifting the flours together). Sprinkle the flours in slowly, then add the egg whites, beaten to stiff peaks.

2 Mix well, then spread the mixture on a baking sheet covered with aluminum foil, lightly buttered and sprinkled with potato flour. Bake at 250°F for about 15 minutes, then remove the dessert and turn it out onto a flat surface that you have sprinkled with coarse sugar.

3 Place the chestnut cream in a bowl and mix it with a tablespoon rum and the melted butter, then evenly spread the mixture on the surface of the prepared dessert.

4 Roll it up and, being careful not to break it, slide it onto a serving dish. Let it cool at room temperature for at least 4–5 hours, then slice and serve.

Practical Suggestions

You can serve the chestnut roll garnished with dabs of whipped cream on the serving dish. This recipe can also be prepared with any other fruit jam you like.

INGREDIENTS

serves 4

6 EGG YOLKS
2 3/4 cups – 250 g SUGAR
2 teaspoons VANILLA
1/2 cup – 60 g WHITE FLOUR
1 cup – 120 g POTATO FLOUR
6 EGG WHITES, beaten to stiff peaks
2 tablespoons COARSE SUGAR
6 tablespoons CHESTNUT CREAM
1 tablespoon RUM
1 tablespoon MELTED BUTTER

EQUIPMENT

an electric beater
a mixing bowl
a bowl, a baking sheet
aluminum foil
a serving dish

Difficulty	**AVERAGE**
Preparation Time	**30 MIN. + 4 HOURS**
Cooking Time	**15 MIN.**
Method of cooking	**OVEN**
Microwave	**YES**
Freezing	**YES**
Keeping Time	**3 DAYS**

SPECIAL NOTE

In the Veneto area of Italy, shelled and dried chestnuts are known as *straccaganassa* ("jawbreakers"), a reference to the fact that they take some work to chew.

Pistachio Cream Tart

INGREDIENTS

serves 6–8

1/4 lb. – 100 g PISTACHIOS
2 cups – 1/2 liter MILK
5 EGG YOLKS, 1 1/8 cups – 100 g SUGAR
1/3 cup – 40 g WHITE FLOUR
1 teaspoon KIRSCH
1 oz. – 20 g CANDIED CITRON
3/4 lb. – 300 g READY-MADE PUFF PASTRY

For the garnish

1 teaspoon POWDERED SUGAR
2 oz. – 40 g DARK CHOCOLATE
1.5 oz. – 30 g PISTACHIOS

For the quiche pan

1 oz. – 20 g BUTTER
1 oz. – 20 g FLOUR

EQUIPMENT

a small saucepan, a skillet, a quiche pan
vegetable paper, a serving dish

Difficulty	**AVERAGE**
Preparation Time	**30 MIN. + 30 MIN.**
Cooking Time	**50 MIN.**
Method of cooking	**STOVETOP AND OVEN**
Microwave	**NO**
Freezing	**YES**
Keeping Time	**3 DAYS**

SPECIAL NOTE

Arab countries often use toasted pistachios that are commonly consumed as a snack food. They can be bought from traveling vendors.

Recommended Wines

Gioia del Colle Aleatico dolce (Puglia): aged red wine served at 50°F / 10°C
Montefalco Sagrantino passito (Umbria): liqueur–like or dry raisin wine served at 50°F / 10°C

1 Scald the pistachios in a small saucepan of boiling water, drain, skin and mince. Bring the milk to a boil. Mix the egg yolks with the sugar in a skillet until well blended. Add the pistachios and add the flour a little at a time, mixing in the hot milk in a thin stream (stirring constantly). Place the skillet on the heat and bring to a boil, mixing often. Cover, lower the heat to simmer and continue cooking for 7–8 minutes. Remove the skillet from the heat and let the custard cool. Add the kirsch and minced candied citron, and mix in.

2 Roll out the dough and line a buttered, floured quiche pan with it. Poke the bottom with a fork and pour the pistachio custard over it, smoothing evenly. Place in a preheated 350°F oven and bake 25–30 minutes. When done, remove the tart, turn out onto a serving dish and sprinkle with powdered sugar.

3 In the meantime, prepare the decoration. Melt the chocolate over a double boiler. Scald the pistachios in boiling water and skin them. Place the melted chocolate in a cone of vegetable paper, and squeezing, decorate the tart by drawing a tree with numerous branches, and using the halved pistachios to make flowers.

Practical Suggestions

If you like, you can use 1 cup – 125 grams flour, 1/4 cup – 50 grams butter, a half a grated lemon zest, 1/3 cup – 30 grams sugar, an egg yolk, and a teaspoon vanilla to make the tart crust.

Florentine Chestnut Cake

INGREDIENTS

serves 6–8

2 oz. – 50 g RAISINS
3/4 lb. – 300 g CHESTNUT FLOUR
SALT to taste
4 tablespoons SUGAR
6 tablespoons EXTRA VIRGIN OLIVE OIL
2 oz. – 50 g PINE NUTS
a few leaves ROSEMARY

For the cake pan

EXTRA VIRGIN OLIVE OIL as necessary
BREAD CRUMBS as necessary

EQUIPMENT

a small bowl
a mixing bowl
a cake pan
a serving dish

Difficulty	AVERAGE
Preparation Time	10 MIN. + 20 MIN.
Cooking Time	1 HOUR
Method of cooking	OVEN
Microwave	NO
Freezing	NO
Keeping Time	3 DAYS

SPECIAL NOTE

Chestnut cake is a specialty that became popular around the end of the 19th century, spreading from Tuscany to the rest of Italy through makeshift bakeries.

RECOMMENDED WINES

Bianco Pisano di San Torpé Vin Santo (Tuscany): liqueur–like wine or dry raisin wine served at 50°F / 10°C

Albana di Romagna dolce (Emilia Romagna): liqueur–like wine or dry raisin wine served at 50°F / 10°C

1 Plump the raisins for 20 minutes in a small bowl of lukewarm water, then drain, squeeze and set aside. Place the chestnut flour in a mixing bowl, add a pinch of salt and the sugar, mix well with a wooden spoon to blend the ingredients, then add 4 tablespoons oil.

2 Carefully blend everything and, stirring constantly with a wooden spoon, gradually add enough lukewarm water to make a fluid, uniform batter.

3 Lightly oil a cake pan, sprinkle with bread crumbs and pour in the batter. Smooth the surface with a spatula and sprinkle with the pine nuts and raisins. If you like the flavor, add a few rosemary leaves. Finally, drizzle with the remaining oil.

4 Bake in a preheated 350°F oven for about an hour. When done, remove from the oven, transfer to a serving dish and serve.

PRACTICAL SUGGESTIONS

Chestnut cake should be baked and consumed immediately, while it is piping hot. When eaten cold or reheated, it loses much of its flavor. Chestnut flour may be made by grinding dried chestnuts in a food mill or processor.

Apricot Torte

INGREDIENTS

serves 6

1 lb. – 500 g APRICOTS
1/2 cup – 100 g BUTTER
4 EGGS
1 1/2 cups – 150 g SUGAR
1 teaspoon VANILLA
1 cup – 120 g FLOUR
2 teaspoons BAKING POWDER
1 tablespoon GRATED BREAD CRUMBS

EQUIPMENT

a bowl
a quiche pan
a serving dish

Difficulty	AVERAGE
Preparation Time	1 HOUR + 10 MIN.
Cooking Time	40 MIN.
Method of cooking	OVEN
Microwave	YES
Freezing	YES
Keeping Time	3 DAYS

SPECIAL NOTE

Apricots are a true treasure-trove of vitamin A. They can also strengthen the eyes and improve night vision, and help the skin tan more easily.

Recommended Wines

Trentino Vin Santo (Trentino Alto Adige): liqueur–like wine or dry raisin wine served at 50°F / 10°C

Malvasia delle Lipari (Sicily): aged red wine served at 50°F / 10°C

1 Wash the apricots, dry them, remove the pits and cut into rings about a half an inch – 1 centimeter thick. Cut the butter into pieces, place in a bowl and soften to room temperature. Then mash it a bit with a wooden spoon and add the egg yolks one at a time (setting the whites aside), stirring constantly. Add the sugar and vanilla and mix until you have a uniform, foamy mixture.

2 Add the flour sifted with the baking powder and mix, blending the ingredients well, then gently fold in the egg whites, beaten to stiff peaks.

3 Pour two thirds of the mixture into the quiche pan (which you have buttered and sprinkled with grated bread crumbs), then add a layer of apricot rings. Cover with the remaining mixture and add the remaining apricots.

4 Bake in a preheated 375°F oven for about 40 minutes. When done, remove and turn out onto a serving dish. Allow it to cool completely before serving.

Practical Suggestions

If the apricots are not fully ripe, you can steam them for 3–4 minutes to soften them. To make them even more flavorful, you can briefly cook them in sugar syrup.

Raspberry Sand Cake

INGREDIENTS

serves 6–8

1 1/4 cup – 150 g WHITE FLOUR
2 oz. – 50 g ALMONDS, shelled and ground
1/2 cup – 40 g SUGAR
1/3 cup – 70 g BUTTER
1 EGG YOLK
a tablespoon GRATED LEMON ZEST
4 tablespoons RASPBERRY GELATIN
1 lb. – 500 g RASPBERRIES

EQUIPMENT

a small saucepan
a spring mold about 10 inches – 24 cm in diameter
baking parchment
a handful of dry beans
a serving dish

Difficulty	**AVERAGE**
Preparation Time	**45 MIN. + 30 MIN.**
Cooking Time	**25 MIN.**
Method of cooking	**OVEN**
Microwave	**NO**
Freezing	**YES**
Keeping Time	**3 DAYS**

SPECIAL NOTE

Raspberries grow wild all over Europe and are cultivated in Germany, Great Britain and France, as well as Poland and Hungary, which offer fruit for industrial use.

RECOMMENDED WINES

Verdicchio dei Castelli di Jesi passito (Marche): liqueur–like wine or dry raisin wine served at 50°F / 10°C

Aleatico di Gradoli (Lazio): liqueur–like wine or dry raisin wine served at 50°F / 10°C

1 Sift the flour, add the almonds and sugar, mound it and place the softened, chopped butter in the center along with the egg yolks and lemon zest. Quickly make the dough, then wrap in a damp cloth and let it sit in a cool place for 30 minutes.

2 Remove the dough and roll it out to about 1/8 inch, then use it to line the buttered, floured quiche pan. Poke the bottom with a fork, cover with a sheet of baking parchment and fill it with dry beans.

3 Bake the shell in a preheated 375°F oven for about 20 minutes, then remove the vegetable paper and beans and continue cooking for a few minutes until it is golden. Remove and cool.

4 Bring the raspberry gelatin to a boil in a small saucepan with a tablespoon water, mix and remove from the heat. Place the tart on a serving dish, brush the bottom with the lukewarm gelatin and place the raspberries on top, arranged in concentric circles. Brush with the remaining gelatin and serve.

PRACTICAL SUGGESTIONS

To avoid wasting the very delicate flesh of raspberries, it's best to remove the stem after washing and drying them. Instead of picking them up with your hands, use a toothpick to handle them.

Melon Puff Pastry Dessert

INGREDIENTS

serves 6

1/3 lb. – 150 g FROZEN PUFF PASTRY
or phyllo dough
2 oz. – 50 g DRY PLAIN COOKIES
1 MELON weighing about 1 3/4 lb. – 700 g
3/4 cup – 70 g SUGAR
a VANILLA bean

For the finish

2 oz. – 50 g APRICOT GELATIN

EQUIPMENT

a rolling pin
a quiche pan about 10 inches in diameter
a skillet
a small saucepan
a serving dish

Difficulty	**AVERAGE**
Preparation Time	**20 MIN.**
Cooking Time	**40 MIN.**
Method of cooking	**STOVETOP AND OVEN**
Microwave	**NO**
Freezing	**YES**
Keeping Time	**3 DAYS**

SPECIAL NOTE

Three types of melons will do: cantaloupe, which are spherical and have a thick, rough skin; musk melons, which are more oval, with a thin skin; and honeydew melons, with a smooth skin and pale green or white flesh.

RECOMMENDED WINES

Collio Goriziano Picolit (Friuli–Venezia Giulia): liqueur–like wine or dry raisin wine served at 50°F / 10°C

Malvasia di Bosa (Sardinia): liqueur–like wine or dry raisin wine served at 50°F / 10°C

1 Using the rolling pin, roll out the pastry to about 1/8 inch thick. Using a small, sharp knife, cut a disk of dough about 10 inches in diameter and place it in the round pan. Brush with a little water, pinch the edges, and poke a number of holes in the bottom with a fork. Crumble the cookies and spread them uniformly over the pastry.

2 Skin the melon and remove the seeds. Chop it into thin, regular slices. Place them in the skillet, add the sugar and vanilla bean, slowly bring to a boil and continue cooking for about 10 minutes. Remove the vanilla bean from the skillet and drain the melon slices. Then make a radiating layer of melon slices on the pastry, overlapping them a little. Form a second, smaller layer in the center, radiating the slices in the opposite direction.

3 Place the pan in a preheated 375°F oven and bake about 25 minutes, until the pastry is a light golden brown. Then remove from the oven and place the pastry in a serving dish. Dissolve the apricot gelatin in a small saucepan with a teaspoon water and brush the melon slices. Serve the pastry lukewarm or cold.

PRACTICAL SUGGESTIONS

When you buy a melon, be sure that it's solid with no soft places, and that the bottom end gives slightly when pressed with your finger.

Apple Bread Pudding

INGREDIENTS
serves 4

3 oz. – 80 g SHELLED ALMONDS
2 oz. – 60 g RAISINS
1 lb. – 400 g BREAD
2 EGGS
1 1/8 cups – 100 g SUGAR
pinch of SALT
zest of one LEMON
1 cup MILK
1 1/2 lb. – 600 g APPLES
1/4 cup – 60 g BUTTER

EQUIPMENT

a small saucepan
a bowl
a mixing bowl
a cake pan
a serving dish

Difficulty	AVERAGE
Preparation Time	20 MIN. + 20 MIN.
Cooking Time	40 MIN.
Method of cooking	STOVETOP
Microwave	YES
Freezing	NO
Keeping Time	2 DAYS

SPECIAL NOTE

The best time of the day to eat apples is after main meals, because not only do they help digestion, but the oxalic acid in them also whitens the teeth.

RECOMMENDED WINES

Moscadello di Montalcino (Tuscany): liqueur–like wine or dry raisin wine served at 50°F / 10°C

Malvasia delle Lipari (Sicily): liqueur–like wine or dry raisin wine served at 50°F / 10°C

1 Immerse the almonds in a small saucepan of boiling water for a few minutes, then drain, peel carefully, dry and sliver. Soak the raisins in a bowl of lukewarm water for 20 minutes, then drain and squeeze well.

2 Slice the bread thinly. Break the eggs into a mixing bowl, add the sugar and beat well with the whip until you have an almost white foam. Then add the salt and a grated lemon zest, blend in the milk, pouring it in a thin stream, and continue to mix with a wooden spoon until you have a uniform mixture.

3 Wash the apples, peel, remove the core and slice. Butter the bottom and sides of a cake pan with a third of the butter and place alternating layers of bread, apple slices, egg mixture, slivered almonds, raisins and the remaining butter, dotted on.

4 Bake in a preheated 350°F oven for 35–40 minutes, then remove, transfer to a serving dish and serve lukewarm or cold, as you like.

PRACTICAL SUGGESTIONS

This simple but delicious dessert can be served with liquid cream served in a separate creamer. The best apples for this recipe are Golden Delicious, and the bread can be an ordinary square loaf.

Gubana

Recommended Wines

Colli Orientali del Friuli Cialla Picolit (Friuli Venezia Giulia): liqueur–like wine or dry raisin wine served at 54°F / 12°C

Moscadello di Montalcino (Tuscany): liqueur–like wine or dry raisin wine served at 54°F / 12°C

1 Soak the sultana and zibibbo raisins in the marsala for about 20 minutes. Using a chopping knife, mince the walnuts, figs, prunes, and citron, and place in a mixing bowl with the well–squeezed sultana and zibibbo raisins, pine nuts, pineapple, chocolate and grated citrus rinds.

2 In a small frying pan, sauté the grated bread crumbs in the butter for a bit, then add this to the other ingredients as well. Mix everything well with a wooden spoon, then add the egg yolk and the white, beaten to stiff peaks.

3 Put the packages of pastry together, then roll them with the rolling pin until you have a thick sheet, which you should flour a bit. Place the prepared filling in the center, then wrap it into a long roll. Place it on a buttered baking sheet, rolled up into a spiral.

4 Lightly beat the egg yolk and brush the surface of the dessert with it, then bake in a preheated 350°F oven for about 45 minutes. When done, remove, sprinkle the surface with the vanilla–flavored sugar and serve.

Practical Suggestions

In the Veneto and Friuli areas of Italy, gubana is prepared with yeasted sweet pastry, or strudel dough, which is a lightly sweetened noodle dough.

INGREDIENTS

serves 6

1/4 lb. – 100 g SULTANA RAISINS
1/4 lb. – 100 g ZIBIBBO RAISINS (very sweet raisins from muscat grapes)
1 cup SWEET MARSALA WINE
1/3 lb. – 125 g WALNUT KERNELS
4 DRIED FIGS, 4 PRUNES
1.5 oz. – 30 g CANDIED CITRON
2 oz. – 50 g PINE NUTS
2 SLICES CANNED PINEAPPLES, diced
2 oz. – 50 g BAKER'S CHOCOLATE, chopped
zest of one LEMON and one ORANGE,
2 oz. – 50 g GRATED BREAD CRUMBS
1/3 cup – 60 g BUTTER, 1 EGG YOLK, 1 EGG
2 PACKAGES FROZEN PUFF PASTRY or phyllo dough
1 tablespoon VANILLA–FLAVORED SUGAR

EQUIPMENT

a baking sheet, a bowl
a mixing bowl, a small frying pan

Difficulty	**ELABORATE**
Preparation Time	**1 HOUR**
Cooking Time	**45 MIN.**
Method of cooking	**OVEN**
Microwave	**NO**
Freezing	**YES**
Keeping Time	**7 DAYS**

SPECIAL NOTE

Gubana is very high in calories due to its high sugar and fat content. It is thus good for anyone who needs to gain weight.

Spoon Desserts

Frosty Oranges with Sorbet

INGREDIENTS
serves 4

1 1/4 cups – 125 g SUGAR
4 ORANGES
half an EGG WHITE

For the garnish
1.5 oz. – 30 g CANDIED ORANGE
5 tablespoons – 1 dl WHIPPED CREAM

EQUIPMENT
a skillet
a corer
a vegetable mill
a mixing bowl
an ice cream machine
a pastry bag with fluted tip

Difficoltà	AVERAGE
Preparation Time	40 MIN.
Cooking Time	10 MIN.
Method of cooking	STOVETOP
Microwave	NO
Freezing	YES
Keeping Time	1 DAY

SPECIAL NOTE
The word orange comes from the Persian *narang*, and in fact oranges come from the Far East. Today some of the best, sweetest and juiciest oranges ripen under the Sicilian sun.

RECOMMENDED WINES
Alto Adige Moscato giallo (Trentino Alto Adige): liqueur–like wine or sweet raisin wine served at 50°F / 10°C
Oltrepò Pavese Moscato (Lombardy): aged red wine served at 50°F / 10°C

1 Place half a cup water in a skillet with the sugar, bring to a boil and boil about 10 minutes. Remove the syrup from the heat and let it cool completely. In the meantime, wash and dry the oranges. Remove the stems, and using a small curved knife and a corer, separate the oranges from their rinds. Discard the white skin, being careful not to break the rinds, and place the emptied oranges in the freezer.

2 Run the orange pulp through the vegetable mill. Weigh out 3/4 lb. – 300 g of the puree and place in a mixing bowl, add the syrup and mix. Pour the mixture into the ice cream machine and set according to the instructions. When half the time has passed, add the lightly beaten egg white, and complete the preparation.

3 Remove the emptied oranges from the freezer and fill with the sorbet you have just prepared. Return to the freezer for about 30 minutes or until ready to serve. In the meantime, prepare the garnish. Using a small, sharp knife, cut the candied orange into very thin strips. When ready to serve, place the whipped cream in the pastry bag and make rosettes on the surface of the sorbet. Place the candied orange strips on top of the whipped cream.

PRACTICAL SUGGESTIONS
If you don't have an ice cream machine, put the mixture in a wide, shallow, stainless steel container. Cover with plastic wrap and leave in the freezer about 3 hours, mixing at 30 minute intervals.

Blueberry Mousse

Recommended Wines

Gambarella Recioto (Veneto): liqueur–like wine or dry raisin wine served at 46°F / 8°C

Asti Spumante (Piedmont): dry sparkling wine served at 46°F / 8°C

1 Carefully wash the blueberries in ice water, dry gently, run through a vegetable mill and place the puree in the refrigerator. Wash the lemon, dry it, and using a potato peeler, remove the yellow part of the rind. Then squeeze the lemon and set the juice aside.

2 Bring a half a quart – half a liter of water to boil in a small saucepan with the lemon rind and butter. Blend the egg yolks with the sugar in a skillet, until you have a white, foamy mixture. Then add the flour, and slowly add the water and butter mixture after removing the lemon rind.

3 Place the skillet on the heat and slowly bring to a boil, then continue cooking over low heat for 10 minutes, stirring constantly to prevent the custard from sticking. Remove from the heat, add the blueberry purée and lemon juice, and finally blend in the egg whites, beaten to stiff peaks.

4 Pour the warm mixture into a moistened mold, cool at room temperature, then refrigerate for at least 3 hours. When ready to serve, turn over onto a serving dish and decorate as you like with whipped cream.

Practical Suggestions

You can also use frozen blueberries for this mousse. If you do, defrost them at room temperature and drain. Check to see if they are already sweetened; if so, reduce the sugar by one third.

INGREDIENTS

serves 4–6

1 lb. – 400 g BLUEBERRIES (or bilberries)

1 LEMON

50 oz. – 1/4 cup BUTTER

3 EGGS

1 1/2 cups – 140 g SUGAR

2/3 cup – 80 g FLOUR

For the garnish

WHIPPED CREAM as necessary

EQUIPMENT

a vegetable mill

a small saucepan

a skillet

a 3/4 quart – 3/4 liter mold

a serving dish

Difficulty	**AVERAGE**
Preparation Time	**30 MIN. + 3–4 HOURS**
Cooking Time	**20 MIN.**
Method of cooking	**STOVETOP**
Microwave	**NO**
Freezing	**YES**
Keeping Time	**1 DAY**

SPECIAL NOTE

Bilberries are smooth berries from the wild bilberry bush, a member of the Ericaceae family. The most common variety is the black bilberry, common in woods in the Alps and Apennines, Scandinavia and Germany.

Melon and Raspberry Aspic

INGREDIENTS
serves 6

1 1/8 cups – 100 g SUGAR
1.5 oz. – 30 g SHEET (or powdered) GELATIN softened in abundant cold water
2 cups – half a liter DRY WHITE WINE
3/4 lb. – 300 g RASPBERRIES
1 MELON WEIGHING 1 3/4 lb. – 700 g cleaned and cut into melon balls
1 sliced ORANGE

EQUIPMENT
a skillet
a stainless steel mold
a serving dish

Difficulty	ELABORATE
Preparation Time	40 MIN. + 2 HOURS
Cooking Time	10 MIN.
Method of cooking	STOVETOP
Microonde	NO
Freezing	NO
Keeping Time	2 DAYS

SPECIAL NOTE
Unlike other European countries, especially in Northern Europe, and the United States, raspberries are rarely cultivated in Italy.

RECOMMENDED WINES
Alto Adige Moscato rosé (Trentino Alto Adige): liqueur–like wine or sweet raisin wine served at 46°F / 8°C
Frascati Cannellino Spumante (Lazio): aged red wine served at 46°F / 8°C

1 Place half a quart of water and the sugar in a skillet, bring to a boil, and boil ten minutes. Remove from the heat, add the gelatin, drained and well squeezed. and mix until dissolved. Cool, then add the white wine and mix again. Pour a thin layer of gelatin into the mold and let it harden in the refrigerator. Add a layer of raspberries, pour a bit of gelatin on top and return to the refrigerator again, until the gelatin has almost solidified. Remove the mold from the refrigerator, place a layer of melon balls on it, and add a bit of gelatin to this. Put the mold in the refrigerator until the gelatin has almost solidified. Continue in this way until you have finished the ingredients, being careful not to touch the sides of the mold.

2 Before making the last layer of fruit, place the sliced oranges all around the edge, with half the orange resting on the edge of the mold and half sticking out of the mold. Form the last layer of fruit, and fill with the gelatin to barely cover. Place the mold in the refrigerator, and when the gelatin has almost solidified, turn the half slices of orange back over it. Finally, finish with a final layer of gelatin, and refrigerate the mold for 2 hours. When ready to serve, immerse the mold in hot water and turn out the aspic onto a serving dish.

PRACTICAL SUGGESTIONS
When you buy the raspberries, make sure they are whole and dry. Liquid on the bottom means that the fruit underneath will be soft and sour, or at the best crushed.

Moscovite Gelato

INGREDIENTS

serves 4

1 LEMON
rind of one ORANGE
1 1/3 cups – 125 g SUGAR
scant 1 lb. – 350 g STRAWBERRIES
1 slice minced PINEAPPLE
1 cup ORANGE juice
half an EGG WHITE

For the garnish

7 STRAWBERRIES
5 tablespoons – 1 dl WHIPPED CREAM

EQUIPMENT

a saucepan, a blender
a mixing bowl, a bowl
an ice cream machine, a mold
a pastry bag with fluted tip
a serving dish

Difficulty	**AVERAGE**
Preparation Time	**40 MIN. + 30 MIN.**
Cooking Time	**5 MIN.**
Method of cooking	**STOVETOP**
Microonde	**NO**
Freezing	**YES**
Keeping Time	**1 DAY**

SPECIAL NOTE

Strawberry juice is used in creams and tonics for the skin, and the fruit pulp is used for beauty masks.

RECOMMENDED WINES

Oltrepò Pavese Moscato liquoroso dolce (Lombardy): liqueur–like wine or dry raisin wine served at 50°F / 10°C

Campi Flegrei Piedirosso passito (Campania): liqueur–like wine or dry raisin wine served at 54°F / 12°C

1 Wash the lemon, remove the peel and squeeze half the lemon. Wash an orange and remove the rind, then cut the 2 rinds into thin strips. Pour 3/4 cup – 1.5 dl water in a saucepan, add the sugar, place over the heat and boil until the sugar is dissolved. Remove from the heat and cool. Wash the strawberries, dry them and remove the stems. Place in the blender, add the lemon, and whip. Then put through a sieve, and place the puree in a mixing bowl. Add the pineapple, the strips of orange and lemon rind and the orange juice. Let it sit for about 30 minutes and add the sugar syrup. Run everything through the sieve and place in a bowl, then transfer to an ice cream machine and set according to the instructions.

2 When half the indicated time has passed, add the egg white and complete the preparation. Transfer the gelato to a metal mold and place in the freezer until ready to serve. In the meantime, prepare the garnish. Wash the strawberries, remove the stems and slice some thinly and others into wedges. When ready to serve, turn gelato out onto a serving dish. Place the cream into a pastry bag and decorate the base of the gelato and the top. Insert the strawberry wedges between one rosette of whipped cream and another, place the slices on the top, and end with a last rosette of whipped cream.

PRACTICAL SUGGESTIONS

The time required to prepare a good gelato may vary. It depends on the mixture prepared (how much fat and how much sugar the recipe contains). The fattier and sweeter the mixture, the more time will be required.

Strawberry Cups

INGREDIENTS
serves *6–8*

1 cup – 100 g TAPIOCA
1/4 cup – 1 dl MILK
1/8 cup – 30 g BUTTER
7 tablespoons SUGAR
1 teaspoon VANILLA
2 EGGS
1/2 cup – 2 dl CREAM
1 1/2 lb. – 600 g STRAWBERRIES
a few spoonfuls KIRSCH

EQUIPMENT
2 mixing bowls
a skillet
a double boiler
6–8 serving cups

Difficulty	AVERAGE
Preparation Time	20 MIN. + 2 HOURS
Cooking Time	30 MIN.
Method of cooking	STOVETOP
Microonde	NO
Freezing	NO
Keeping Time	1 DAY

SPECIAL NOTE
Tapioca is prepared from manioc flour; when moist, it is run through a very fine sieve, and the resulting granules are dried on a sheet at 212°F – 100°C.

RECOMMENDED WINES

Collio Goriziano Picolit (Friuli–Venezia Giulia): liqueur–like wine or dry raisin wine served at 50°F / 10°C

Moscato di Sorso Sennori (Sardinia): liqueur–like wine or dry raisin wine served at 50°F / 10°C

1 Place the tapioca in a mixing bowl and cover with cold water, being sure it is completely immersed. Leave it for an hour, then drain and place in a skillet.

2 Add the cold milk and the butter, and stirring continuously, cook over a double boiler until the tapioca becomes transparent. Then add the sugar and vanilla, then the lightly beaten eggs, place everything back on the heat over the double boiler, and continue cooking until the custard thickens. Let it cool, then mix in the cream, which you have whipped in a separate mixing bowl.

3 Wash the strawberries well, slice and soak a few minutes in a bowl with the kirsch, then drain and place them in the serving cups, alternating in layers with the prepared custard. Refrigerate the cups for at least an hour before serving.

PRACTICAL SUGGESTIONS

If you can't find tapioca, you can use an equal amount of corn starch instead. You can also prepare these delicious fruit cups with other types of fruit, like blueberries, raspberries, alpine strawberries, blackberries or kiwis.

Apricot Flan

INGREDIENTS

serves 4

2 lb. – 800 g firm, ripe APRICOTS
2 1/4 cups – 200 g SUGAR
1 cup NATURAL WHITE MUSCATEL WINE
4 EGGS
a walnut–sized chunk BUTTER

EQUIPMENT

a skillet
a vegetable mill
a saucepan
a mixing bowl
a ring–shaped mold
aluminum foil
a serving dish

Difficulty	AVERAGE
Preparation Time	15 MIN.
Cooking Time	1 HOURS
Method of cooking	STOVETOP AND OVEN
Microonde	NO
Freezing	NO
Keeping Time	1 DAY

SPECIAL NOTE

Apricots are now considered an excellent, healthful fruit primarily because of their vitamins and mineral salts. In fact, despite the sweetness of the pulp, they contain no more than 6–7% sugars.

RECOMMENDED WINES

Alto Adige Moscato rosa (Trentino Alto Adige): liqueur–like wine or sweet raisin wine served at 50°F / 10°C

Nasco di Cagliari dolce (Sardinia): aged red wine served at 50°F / 10°C

1 Wash the apricots, dry them with a dishtowel and remove the pits. Place in a skillet, sprinkle with sugar and soak in the muscatel wine.

2 Place the skillet over moderate heat and cook the apricots for about 15 minutes, stirring occasionally with a wooden spoon. Run through the vegetable mill, place the puree in a saucepan and boil off the remaining liquid, continuing to stir.

3 Remove the saucepan from the heat, pour the puree into a mixing bowl and let it cool. Then add the eggs one at a time and mix well.

4 Butter a ring mold, pour in the mixture, cover with aluminum foil and cook over a double boiler in a preheated 350°F oven for 40–45 minutes.

5 Remove the mold from the oven, run the blade of a knife along the edges of the mold to loosen the dessert, turn over onto a serving dish and decorate. Serve either lukewarm or cold.

PRACTICAL SUGGESTIONS

You can decorate this dessert with a few slices of apricot (as shown in the photo) or garnish with dabs of whipped cream.

Cherry Sorbet

INGREDIENTS

serves 4

1 LEMON
1 lb. – 500 g CHERRIES
2 tablespoons KIRSCH
1 1/8 cup – 100 g SUGAR
half an EGG WHITE

EQUIPMENT

a small bowl
a pot
a blender
a frying pan
a wide skillet with high sides
an ice cream machine
4 serving cups

Difficulty	**AVERAGE**
Preparation Time	**20 MIN. + 30 MIN.**
Cooking Time	**7 MIN.**
Method of cooking	**STOVETOP**
Microonde	**NO**
Freezing	**YES**
Keeping Time	**3 DAYS**

SPECIAL NOTE

Because they are low in calories, cherries are an ideal light snack for in between meals. Rich in water and sugars, they also have a high vitamin and mineral content.

Recommended Wines

Colli di Parma Malvasia Spumante (Emilia–Romagna): aged red wine served at 46°F / 8°C

Malvasia di Casorzo d'Asti Spumante (Piedmont): aged red wine served at 46°F / 8°C

1 Wash the lemon, dry it, remove the zest (only the yellow portion, which you should set aside), squeeze it and place the juice in a small bowl. Wash the cherries well, drain and pit (you should end up with 3/4 lb. or a little more – 300–350 grams). Place in a casserole, add the juice and lemon zest and cook 3–4 minutes over high heat, stirring occasionally with a wooden spoon.

2 Remove from the heat, drain the cherries well, remove the lemon zest and let the cherries cool. Then run through the blender until you have a uniform mixture. Add the kirsch. Place 1/4 cup – 1 dl liter water in a skillet with the sugar, slowly bring to a boil and boil 2–3 minutes, until the sugar is completely dissolved, then remove from the heat and cool completely.

3 When cooled, add the cherry purée and mix with a wooden spoon, until it is completely blended with the other ingredients. Pour the mixture into the ice cream machine and set it according to the instructions. When half the required time has passed, add the egg white and finish preparing. When the sorbet is ready, place into individual cups and serve.

Practical Suggestions

When you serve the sorbet, place it in the cups with the spatula or use an ice cream scooper. If you use a scooper, always dip it in water for easier scooping. Try to work quickly so the sorbet doesn't melt.

Mango Parfait

INGREDIENTS
serves 8

3/4 lb. – 350 g MANGOES
1 3/4 cup – 150 g SUGAR
5 EGG YOLKS
2 cups – half a liter WHIPPED CREAM

For decoration
1/4 cup – 1 dl WHIPPED CREAM

EQUIPMENT
a blender
a small saucepan
a saucepan
a mixing bowl
an electric beater
a stainless steel mold
a serving dish

Difficulty	**AVERAGE**
Preparation Time	**20 MIN. + 2 HOURS**
Cooking Time	**20 MIN.**
Method of cooking	**STOVETOP**
Microonde	**NO**
Freezing	**YES**
Keeping Time	**3 DAYS**

SPECIAL NOTE
Mangoes are the exotic fruit of the mango tree *(Mangifera indica)*, a member of the Anacardiaceae family, indigenous to Malaysia. It is reddish–green, with a smooth skin, and orange pulp.

RECOMMENDED WINES
Moscato d'Asti (Piedmont): aged red wine served at 46°F / 8°C
Moscato di Pantelleria (Sicily): aged red wine served at 46°F / 8°C

1 Peel the mango, and using a small, well-sharpened knife, cut the pulp into pieces. Place it in the blender (setting aside about 2 ounces for decoration), add 1/2 cup sugar and whip until you have a uniform mixture. Place in a small saucepan, bring it gently to a boil, and reduce it by a third over moderate heat, stirring continuously with a wooden spoon. Place a cup of water in another saucepan, add the remaining sugar, bring it slowly to a boil, and continue cooking another 8–10 minutes, until the syrup is quite thick and transparent.

2 In the meantime, beat the egg yolks in a mixing bowl until they have become clear and fluffy. Pour in the hot syrup in a thin stream and blend it in, beating quickly with the electric mixer. Then add the mango mixture and cool, stirring constantly. Finally, blend in the whipped cream.

3 Place the mixture into a stainless steel mold and freeze for at least 2 hours. When ready to serve, immerse the mold in hot water for a moment. Then turn out the parfait on a serving dish, slice, and decorate with dabs of whipped cream and the pieces of mango you set aside.

PRACTICAL SUGGESTIONS
Fresh cream whips more easily if you keep the beaters and container in the freezer until cold. Avoid using ultrapasteurized cream, which requires too much time to whip.

Melon Sorbet

RECOMMENDED WINES

Taburno Spumante (Campania): aged red wine served at 46°F / 8°C
Cagnina di Romagna (Emilia Romagna): served at 54°F / 12°C

1 Place 1/4 cup water and the sugar in a small saucepan. Bring to a boil and boil for 2–3 minutes, until the sugar is completely dissolved, then remove the syrup from the heat and let it cool.

2 In the meantime, chop the melon pulp, place it in the blender and whip. Transfer the mixture to a bowl, add the sugar syrup, mix well and whip in the blender again.

3 Pour the mixture into a low metal container, place in the freezer and let it sit for 2–3 hours. When it is fully frozen, break it into pieces with the tip of a sturdy knife and whip again. If you don't plan to serve it immediately, place in the freezer again.

PRACTICAL SUGGESTIONS

If you want an extra aesthetic touch, serve this dish in cups decorated with thin slices of melon and some finely chopped pistachios.

INGREDIENTS

serves 6

1/4 cup – 1 dl WATER
1 1/8 cup – 100 g SUGAR
3/4 lb. – 300 g MELON PULP

EQUIPMENT

a small saucepan
a bowl
a blender
a shallow metal container

Difficulty	**AVERAGE**
Preparation Time	**45 MIN. + 2–3 HOURS**
Cooking Time	**10 MIN.**
Method of cooking	**STOVETOP**
Microonde	**NO**
Freezing	**YES**
Keeping Time	**3 DAYS**

SPECIAL NOTE

Sorbet was all the rage in 18th century Italy, and professor of medicine Filippo Bandini wrote an entire book about it, *De Sorbetis*, printed in Naples in 1784.

Lemon Mousse with Berries

INGREDIENTS
serves 6–8

For the lemon mousse
1/2 oz. – 10 g SHEET (or powdered) GELATIN
1/4 cup LEMON JUICE, 1/2 cup – 50 g SUGAR
1/2 cup – 2 dl WHIPPING CREAM
2.5 oz. – 60 g EGG WHITES

For the berry sauce
1/4 lb. – 100 g STRAWBERRIES
1/4 lb. – 100 g BLACKBERRIES
3/4 cup – 70 g SUGAR

For the garnish
BERRIES of your choosing

EQUIPMENT
a bowl, a small saucepan, a blender
a mold, a sauce boat
a serving dish

Difficulty	**AVERAGE**
Preparation Time	**25 MIN. + 3 HOURS**
Cooking Time	**10 MIN.**
Method of cooking	**STOVETOP**
Microonde	**NO**
Freezing	**YES**
Keeping Time	**2 DAYS**

SPECIAL NOTE
In addition to the more commonly known blackberries, there are also mulberries, which may be dark or light, and have a sweeter taste than blackberries.

RECOMMENDED WINES
Malvasia delle Lipari passito (Sicily): liqueur–like wine or dry raisin wine served at 54°F / 12°C
Montefalco Sagrantino passito (Umbria): liqueur–like wine or dry raisin wine served at 54°F / 12°C

1 Soften the gelatin in a bowl of cold water. In the meantime, bring the lemon juice and the sugar to a boil in a small saucepan, stirring occasionally, and let it boil until the sugar has completely dissolved.

2 Remove the pan from the heat, add the drained, squeezed gelatin and dissolve, stirring often, then cool completely. Whip the cream and gently fold it into the cold mixture. Beat the egg whites to stiff peaks and add them, mixing well. Pour everything in a mold brushed with water and refrigerate at least 3 hours.

3 Prepare the sauce. Wash the strawberries and blackberries gently in ice water, drain, remove the stems and dry gently. Place the fruit in the blender with the sugar, and whip. Sieve the resulting cream and then pour into a sauce boat.

4 When ready to serve, remove the mold from the refrigerator, immerse in hot water for a moment, turn over onto a serving dish, and serve with the berry sauce.

PRACTICAL SUGGESTIONS
To add a touch of color, you can use berries to garnish the edges and center of this dessert, as shown in the photo. If you like, you can also add blueberries and raspberries to the sauce.

Apples with Yogurt

INGREDIENTS

serves 4

4 APPLES
1/4 cup – 20 g SUGAR
1 pinch CINNAMON
4 containers BANANA YOGURT

EQUIPMENT

a small bowl
a baking sheet
aluminum foil
4 serving cups

Difficulty	AVERAGE
Preparation Time	10 MIN.
Cooking Time	15 MIN.
Method of cooking	OVEN
Microonde	YES
Freezing	NO
Keeping Time	2 DAYS

SPECIAL NOTE

Yogurt is a true natural purifier that helps regulate intestinal flora. It makes fats more digestible and absorbs them, and reduces gastric acidity.

RECOMMENDED WINES

Oltrepò Pavese Moscato liquoroso (Lombardy): liqueur–like wine or dry raisin wine served at 50°F / 10°C
Castel San Lorenzo Moscato spumante (Campania): aged red wine served at 46°F / 8°C

1 Wash and dry the apples well, then, using a small, well–sharpened knife, peel, core and cut into quarters. Mix the sugar with the cinnamon in a small bowl.

2 Cover the baking sheet with aluminum foil, place the sliced apples on it and sprinkle with the sugar and cinnamon mixture you prepared.

3 Place the preparation in a preheated 350°F oven and cook the apples for 15–20 minutes (if they seem to be falling apart, remove them sooner).

4 Remove the baking sheet and place two apple quarters in each cup. As soon as the apples have cooled to lukewarm, add the container of yogurt to each cup and serve.

PRACTICAL SUGGESTIONS

To prepare this quick dessert, you can also use raw cane sugar or two teaspoons honey. The banana yogurt can be substituted with strawberry yogurt if you prefer. If you like, you can serve it with a few finger biscuits or ladyfingers.

Mandarin Bavarian Cream

INGREDIENTS

serves 6

1/2 oz. – 10 g SHEET (or powdered) GELATIN
1 cup – 1/4 liter MILK
3 MANDARIN ORANGES
(the juice and grated rind)
4 EGG YOLKS
1 1/8 cup – 100 g SUGAR
6 oz. – 200 g WHIPPED CREAM

EQUIPMENT

a bowl
a skillet
a mixing bowl
a small saucepan
a mold
a serving dish

Difficulty	AVERAGE
Preparation Time	20 MIN. + 2 HOURS
Cooking Time	20 MIN.
Method of cooking	STOVETOP
Microonde	NO
Freezing	NO
Keeping Time	1 DAY

SPECIAL NOTE

Mandarin oranges have about one-third as much vitamin C as oranges. They also have much fewer calories: 7–8 calories per 1/4 pound – 100 grams of fruit.

RECOMMENDED WINES

Vin Santo del Chianti Classico (Tuscany): liqueur–like wine or dry raisin wine served at 54°F / 12°C
Greco di Bianco (Calabria): liqueur–like wine or dry raisin wine served at 50°F / 10°C

1 Soften the gelatin in a bowl of cold water. Heat the milk in a small saucepan and add half the grated mandarin rind. Using a wooden spoon, beat the egg yolks with the sugar in a mixing bowl, until they become foamy and clear. Add the mandarin–flavored hot milk a little at a time.

2 Pour the mixture into a skillet, place it over the heat, add the gelatin, drain and squeeze, then bring to a boil, stirring constantly to prevent the custard from sticking to the pan. Remove from the heat and let it cool, then add the mandarin juice and the remaining grated peel.

3 Gently fold in the whipped cream, then place the mixture into a damp mold and refrigerate for at least 2 hours. Before serving, immerse the mold in hot water for a moment. Turn the Bavarian cream over onto a serving dish and refrigerate again for a few minutes.

PRACTICAL SUGGESTIONS

You can serve this delicious Bavarian cream with a garnish of the segments of two mandarin oranges arranged around the center and base (as shown in the photo).

Autumn Aspic

INGREDIENTS

serves 4

1.5 oz. – 30 g SHEET (or powdered) GELATIN
1/3 lb. – 150 g GREEN GRAPES
1/3 lb. – 150 g PURPLE GRAPES
1/2 lb. – 200 g STRAWBERRIES
2 BANANAS
juice of half a LEMON
1 1/8 cups – 100 g SUGAR
2 cups – half a liter ORANGE JUICE

EQUIPMENT

a mixing bowl
a saucepan
a ring mold
a serving dish

Difficulty	AVERAGE
Preparation Time	20 MIN. + 2 HOURS
Cooking Time	10 MIN.
Method of cooking	STOVETOP
Microonde	NO
Freezing	NO
Keeping Time	3 DAYS

SPECIAL NOTE

Bananas are a very important food source for indigenous peoples in tropical countries. In addition to being a food staple, its leaves are used as containers, plates, bedding, and even roofs.

RECOMMENDED WINES

Oltrepò Pavese Malvasia (Lombardy): aged red wine served at 50°F / 10°C
Colli Euganei Fior d'Arancio (Veneto) served at 50°F / 10°C

1 Soften the gelatin in a mixing bowl of cold water. Wash the grapes, dry them, cut them in half and remove the seeds. Wash the strawberries, dry them and slice. Peel the bananas, cut into rounds and drizzle with the lemon juice.

2 Pour a half a quart – half a liter water and the sugar into a saucepan, slowly bring to a boil, and cook about 10 minutes. Remove the pan from the heat, add the drained, squeezed gelatin and mix well with a wooden spoon until completely dissolved. Let the mixture firm, then pour in the orange juice and mix again.

3 Pour a thin layer of gelatin into the mold and let it solidify in the refrigerator, add a layer of mixed fruit, pour a little gelatin on it and again place it in the refrigerator until the gelatin has firmed. Continue in this manner until you have finished the fruit and gelatin. Finally, place the mold in the refrigerator for at least 2 hours. When ready to serve, immerse the mold in hot water, turn over the aspic onto a serving dish and garnish as you like with mint leaves.

PRACTICAL SUGGESTIONS

Aspic must be served very cold, accompanied, if you like, by small pastries or cookies like ladyfingers. The fruit can vary according to the season. For example, you can use five slices of pineapple, some pitted cherries, or kiwis instead of the strawberries. Use your imagination.

Orange Soup

INGREDIENTS

serves 4

6 ORANGES
1 1/8 cup – 100 g SUGAR
3 oz. – 60 g GLAZED HAZELNUTS

EQUIPMENT

a potato peeler
a small saucepan
a bowl
a saucepan
a serving bowl

Difficulty	AVERAGE
Preparation Time	10 MIN.
Cooking Time	15 MIN.
Method of cooking	STOVETOP
Microonde	NO
Freezing	NO
Keeping Time	2 DAYS

SPECIAL NOTE

Dried, chopped orange peels can be sewn into little bags of perfumed herbs for lingerie. When powdered, they can give an unusual, excellent flavor to bread, cookies, and teas.

RECOMMENDED WINES

Alghero Spumante rosso (Sardinia): aged red wine served at 54°F / 12°C
Carmignano Vin Santo (Tuscany): liqueur–like wine or dry raisin wine served at 54°F / 12°C

1 Wash two oranges, dry them and remove the peel with a potato peeler (being careful to remove only the orange portion. Using a small sharp knife, cut the rind into thin strips and scald them for 2 minutes in a small saucepan of boiling water. Drain, dry and set aside. Squeeze the fruit and place the juice in a bowl.

2 Fully the remaining oranges down to the flesh, being sure to remove the white rind as well, and divide each one into 4 segments. Pour the orange juice into a saucepan, add the sugar, bring it to a boil and boil over moderate heat, until the sugar is completely dissolved.

3 In the meantime, finely mince the glazed hazelnuts, setting aside 4–5 whole nuts. Remove the orange syrup from the heat, add the minced hazelnuts and mix gently. Add the orange segments and strips of boiled rind.

4 Place the saucepan on the heat again and gently bring it to a boil, then remove from the heat. Pour the orange soup into the serving bowl, sprinkle with the nuts you set aside, and serve hot.

PRACTICAL SUGGESTIONS

As you use both the rind and fruit, you should try to find organic oranges for this "soup" if possible. This recipe is also excellent served instead of tea on a winter afternoon.

Frozen Banana Custard

INGREDIENTS

serves 6

4 rather large BANANAS
1/2 cup – 50 g SUGAR
2 ORANGES
half a LEMON
1 pinch POWDERED GINGER
a pinch of SALT
2 tablespoons JAMAICAN RUM

EQUIPMENT

a mixing bowl
an electric beater
individual molds
a serving dish

Difficulty	EASY
Preparation Time	20 MIN. + 2 HOURS
Cooking Time	NO
Method of cooking	NO
Microonde	NO
Freezing	YES
Keeping Time	3 DAYS

SPECIAL NOTE

In folk medicine, bananas were used to heal ulcers. For this purpose, they were cooked very slowly over low heat, to prevent them from losing their therapeutic properties.

Recommended Wines

Aleatico di Puglia dolce naturale (Puglia): aged red wine served at 50°F / 10°C

Colli di Parma Malvasia spumante (Emilia–Romagna): aged red wine served at 46°F / 8°C

1 Peel the bananas and cut into small pieces. Place in a mixing bowl and crush with a fork. Add the sugar, and use a wooden spoon to mix it with the banana pulp, blending the ingredients well.

2 Squeeze the oranges and lemon, and mix the juice with the banana and sugar mixture. Finally, add the ginger, salt and rum.

3 Using an electric beater, beat the mixture until it becomes foamy, Pour into the individual molds and place in the freezer for at least 2 hours.

3 Remove the molds from the freezer 15 minutes before serving the custard, then turn them out on a serving dish and accompany with a rum sauce, or, more simply, with orange segments peeled down to the flesh.

Practical Suggestions

If you don't have molds, put the custard in ice trays without the separators. When it's completely frozen, scoop it by spoonfuls into glass cups, which you can then decorate with slices of orange peeled down to the flesh.

Rice and Peach Mousse

Recommended Wines

Oltrepò Pavese Moscato (Lombardy): aged red wine served at 46°F / 8°C
Bianco di Scandiano frizzante dolce (Emilia–Romagna): aged red wine served at 46°F / 8°C

1 Chop the peaches into cubes and place over the heat in a small skillet with 2 tablespoons peach syrup, 3 tablespoons kirsch and 2 tablespoons sugar. Cook over high heat until the liquid has reduced by 3/4, then turn off the heat. In a pot, slowly boil the milk with the vanilla and the lemon zest. Add the rice, then add the butter and the remaining sugar. Cook slowly until the rice has absorbed all the milk. Then remove the lemon zest and vanilla.

2 Now prepare the custard. Chop the isinglass and soften it for 30 minutes in a bowl with a bit of cold water, then squeeze well. In the meantime, beat the egg yolks in a mixing bowl with the sugar until they become foamy, add the cornstarch, mix and blend with the cream. Cook the custard in a saucepan over very low heat, stirring constantly. As soon as it is cooked and thickened, add the prepared isinglass, stirring rapidly to dissolve completely.

3 Blend 1/3 the cooked peaches with the rice custard. Mix, and as soon as the mixture is tepid, pour into the mold moistened with the remaining kirsch. Place the mousse in a refrigerator for at least 4 hours, then unmold onto a serving dish and fill the hole in the middle with cubed peaches and a few cherries.

Practical Suggestions

*Instead of canned peaches in syrup, you can use 1 lb. – 500 grams fresh peaches that you have peeled and pitted, then cooked for 15 minutes in a small saucepan with water and sugar. *Isinglass is a sheet form of gelatin available now mostly from Asian markets. Powdered gelatin may be substituted.*

INGREDIENTS

serves 4

3/4 lb. – 350 g PEACHES IN SYRUP
5 tablespoons KIRSCH
6 tablespoons SUGAR, 1 VANILLA bean
1 LEMON zest, 1/3 lb. – 160 g RICE
1/8 cup – 30 g BUTTER, 1/4 cup – 1 dl MILK

For the custard

2 sheets ISINGLASS* (or gelatin), 3 EGG YOLKS
3 tablespoons SUGAR
1 tablespoon CORNSTARCH
1/2 cup – 2.5 dl CREAM

For the garnish

CANDIED RED CHERRIES as necessary

EQUIPMENT

a small skillet, a pot, a bowl, 2 mixing bowls, a saucepan, a ring mold, a serving dish

Difficulty	**AVERAGE**
Preparation Time	**20 MIN. + 5 HOURS**
Cooking Time	**50 MIN.**
Method of cooking	**STOVETOP**
Microonde	**NO**
Freezing	**NO**
Keeping Time	**2 DAYS**

SPECIAL NOTE

Vanilla is used as a flavoring for confectionery (custards, sugars, pastries, sweets and sugar–coated almonds), in liqueurs, and to mask the unpleasant taste of medicines.

Apple and Calvados Sorbet

INGREDIENTS
serves 8

3 GRANNY SMITH APPLES
1 1/8 cup – 100 g SUGAR
4 tablespoons LEMON JUICE
3 tablespoons CALVADOS

For the garnish
3/4 cup – 70 g SUGAR

EQUIPMENT
a bowl
a saucepan
a blender
a small saucepan
transparent wrap
a mold
a serving dish

Difficulty	**AVERAGE**
Preparation Time	**40 MIN.**
Cooking Time	**10 MIN.**
Method of cooking	**STOVETOP**
Microonde	**NO**
Freezing	**NO**
Keeping Time	**3 DAYS**

SPECIAL NOTE
Calvados is a French brandy made in the Calvados département of Normandy. It is distilled from apples that are macerated in special mills and then fermented.

RECOMMENDED WINES

Alto Adige moscato giallo (Trentino Alto Adige): liqueur–like wine or sweet raisin wine served at 50°F / 10°C

Gioia del Colle Aleatico dolce (Puglia): liqueur–like wine or dry raisin wine served at 50°F / 10°C

1 Wash the apples and remove the core. Peel, setting the peel aside for the garnish, then chop them all into pieces and put into a bowl, and drizzle with the lemon juice. Pour a cup – a quarter liter of water into a saucepan with the sugar, bring to a boil and boil 2–3 minutes, mixing often, until the sugar is completely dissolved. Remove from the heat and cool. In the meantime, whip the apples and lemon juice in the blender until you have a uniform cream. Sieve and add the syrup and Calvados. Pour the mixture into the ice cream maker and set according to the directions. When done, place the mixture in a mold, cover with transparent wrap and place in the freezer.

2 In the meantime, prepare the garnish. Pour 3 tablespoons water into a small saucepan, add the sugar, place the saucepan on the heat and slowly bring to a boil, stirring until the sugar is completely dissolved and the syrup becomes transparent. Immerse the apple peel you set aside into the syrup, and cook over moderate heat for a minute. Remove from the heat and let it infuse. When ready to serve, remove the sorbet from the freezer and turn out onto a serving dish. Drain the candied peel, roll it a bit, garnish the sorbet with it and serve.

PRACTICAL SUGGESTIONS

You should cover the sorbet with plastic wrap to prevent it from absorbing bad odors. Don't use plastic molds, as they prevent the cold from fully penetrating the sorbet, and it won't become solid enough.

Mandarin Orange Gelatin

INGREDIENTS

serves 4

2 oz. – 40 g SHEET (or powdered) GELATIN
4 cups – 1 liter MANDARIN ORANGE JUICE
2 1/4 cups – 200 g SUGAR
1 small glass RUM
a walnut–sized chunk of BUTTER
4 oz. – 100 g WHIPPED CREAM

EQUIPMENT

a mixing bowl
2 skillets
a sieve
fine mesh gauze
a ring mold
a serving dish

Difficulty	**AVERAGE**
Preparation Time	**15 MIN. + 6 HOURS**
Cooking Time	**10–15 MIN.**
Method of cooking	**STOVETOP**
Microonde	**NO**
Freezing	**NO**
Keeping Time	**2 DAYS**

SPECIAL NOTE

The Chinese prized mandarin oranges and offered them as gifts to mandarins, the officials of the Celestial Empire who gave the fruit its name.

RECOMMENDED WINES

Moscato Passito di Pantelleria (Sicily): liqueur–like wine or dry raisin wine served at 50°F / 10°C

Moscato d'Asti (Piedmont): aged red wine served at 46°F / 8°C

1 Soak the gelatin in a bowl of cold water. Pour one quarter of the mandarin orange juice into a skillet and heat. Place another quarter of the juice in a wide skillet, add the well-squeezed gelatin, the sugar and the heated juice, and cook over low heat.

2 Stir continuously with a wooden spoon until you have completely dissolved both the gelatin and the sugar, then remove the pan from the heat and pour in the remaining cold juice and the rum, and mix well.

3 Butter an approximately quart and a half capacity ring mold, and pour in the liquid, filtering it with a sieve over which you have placed a fine mesh gauze. Cool the preparation and let it chill in the refrigerator for at least 6 hours.

4 Unmold the gelatin on a serving dish, fill the hole in the center with whipped cream, and serve.

PRACTICAL SUGGESTIONS

This gelatin can also be prepared with oranges or tangerines, and you can garnish it with the leaves of whatever fruit you use. If you want, you can use another liquor instead of rum, such as kirsch or maraschino. If you like a milder flavor, use a small glass of mandarin orange liqueur.

Chestnut Semifreddo

INGREDIENTS
serves 4–6

4 EGGS
3/4 cup – 70 g SUGAR
1/4 lb. – 100 g CHESTNUT CREAM
4 tablespoons RUM
4 MARRONS GLACÉS, chopped
1 cup – 1/4 liter WHIPPED CREAM

For the sauce
1 lb. – 400 g PERSIMMONS
2/3 cup – 60 g SUGAR

EQUIPMENT
a mixing bowl
a stainless steel mold
a blender
a serving dish

Difficulty	**AVERAGE**
Preparation Time	**25 MIN. + 2 HOURS**
Cooking Time	**NO**
Method of cooking	**NO**
Microonde	**NO**
Freezing	**YES**
Keeping Time	**3 DAYS**

SPECIAL NOTE
Chestnuts are one of the foods richest in potassium (500 mg per 100 grams), a mineral that is vital to maintain strong muscles.

Recommended Wines
Malvasia di Castelnuovo Don Bosco (Piedmont): aged red wine served at 54°F / 12°C
Colli Orientali del Friuli Ramandolo (Friuli Venezia Giulia): aged red wine served at 50°F / 10°C

1 Beat the egg yolks in a mixing bowl with the sugar (setting the whites aside), until you have a fluffy, foamy mixture. Add the chestnut cream, the rum and the marrons glacés, coarsely chopped, and mix well to blend the ingredients.

2 Beat the egg whites to stiff peaks and fold them delicately into the mixture. Finally, add the whipped cream. Pour the mixture into a stainless steel mold, put into the freezer and let it freeze at least 2 hours.

3 In the meantime, prepare the sauce. Peel the persimmons, remove the seeds and whip with the sugar. Before serving, immerse the mold in hot water for a few moments and then turn out the semifreddo onto a serving dish. Arrange the persimmon sauce around it and decorate with a few marrons glacés.

Practical Suggestions
If you want to make the accompanying sauce more fragrant, add a small cup of Strega liqueur, Campari cordial or Galliano liqueur as you whip it. Marrons glacés are candied chestnuts available at gourmet groceries.

Strawberry Mousse

INGREDIENTS
serves 6–8

1 lb. – 400 g STRAWBERRIES
4 cups – 1 liter MILK
4 sheets ISINGLASS* (or gelatin)
2 1/4 cups – 200 g SUGAR
1 teaspoon VANILLA
2 EGG WHITES
2 cups – half a liter unsweetened WHIPPED CREAM

For the garnish
10 STRAWBERRIES
CREAM as necessary

EQUIPMENT
2 mixing bowls
a skillet
a pudding mold
a serving dish

Difficulty	**AVERAGE**
Preparation Time	**30 MIN. + 4 HOURS**
Cooking Time	**10 MIN.**
Method of cooking	**STOVETOP**
Microonde	**NO**
Freezing	**NO**
Keeping Time	**2 DAYS**

SPECIAL NOTE
Strawberries are especially high in ellagic acid, which is present in both the pulp and the seeds. It is an antioxidant and is sometimes medically used as an intestinal astringent.

RECOMMENDED WINES
Brachetto d'Acqui (Piedmont): aged red wine served at 54°F / 12°C
Oltrepò Pavese Moscato dolce (Lombardy): aged red wine served at 50°F / 10°C

1 Clean the strawberries, put through a sieve and place the purée in a mixing bowl. Place a skillet on the heat with the milk, bring to a boil, then turn off the heat and add the chopped isinglass. Mix well until it dissolves.

2 Filter the milk in a colander, then add the sugar and vanilla, mix again carefully to dissolve the ingredients, and let the preparation cool.

3 In the meantime, in another mixing bowl, beat the egg whites to stiff peaks, then add the cooled milk, the whipped cream and finally the strawberry puree. Be careful to mix from the bottom to the top with a wooden spoon, to prevent the ingredients from losing their fluffiness. Pour everything into the mold and place in the upper part of the refrigerator for at least 3 hours.

4 A few minutes before serving, remove the mold from the refrigerator, immerse in hot water for a few moments and turn out onto a serving dish. Decorate the mousse with the well-washed strawberries and the cream, then serve.

PRACTICAL SUGGESTIONS
You should always buy medium-sized, regularly-formed strawberries with a bright color, firm flesh and strong fragrance. Discard those that are too large, because they will be hollow on the inside, or their pulp will be a bit mealy and sour. **See note on p. 73.*

Green and Purple Grape Mousse

INGREDIENTS

serves 4

4 sheets ISINGLASS* (or gelatin)
4 EGGS
2 cups – 180 g SUGAR
2 tablespoons POTATO FLOUR
1/2 cup – 50 g ALMOND FLOUR
1/2 cup – 2 dl WHITE MARSALA-LIKE WINE
6 tablespoons – 2 dl CREAM
a few large GREEN GRAPES
a few large PURPLE GRAPES
ALMOND OIL as necessary

For the garnish

HONEY as necessary
a few GREEN and PURPLE grapes
GRATED COCONUT as necessary

EQUIPMENT

a bowl, 2 mixing bowls, a skillet
a pudding mold, a serving dish

Difficulty	**AVERAGE**
Preparation Time	**30 MIN. + 3 HOURS**
Cooking Time	**15 MIN.**
Method of cooking	**STOVETOP**
Microonde	**NO**
Freezing	**NO**
Keeping Time	**2 DAYS**

SPECIAL NOTE

A natural remedy for tired skin is to smear some grape pulp on the face fifteen minutes a day. Let the juice dry completely, then rinse.

Recommended Wines

Marsala (Sicily): light sweet wine served at 54°F / 12°C
Caluso passito (Piedmont): liqueur–like wine or dry raisin wine served at 54°F / 12°C

1 Chop the isinglass and let it soften in a bowl with about an inch of cold water. Beat the egg yolks in a mixing bowl with the sugar until you have a foamy, clear mixture. Add the potato flour and the almond flour. Mix well, pour the mixture in a skillet and dilute with white wine. Add the cream, and when everything is well blended, cook over low heat without mixing.

2 When the custard is thickened, remove from the heat and add the well–drained, squeezed isinglass. Add the grapes (which you have thrown into boiling water for a few minutes and then peeled), mix again with a wooden spoon and, spoonful by spoonful, add the egg whites, which you have beaten into stiff peaks in a separate mixing bowl.

3 Oil the mold with the almond oil, pour in the custard and refrigerate the dessert for at least 3 hours. When ready to serve, immerse the bottom of the mold in hot water, then turn out the mousse onto a serving dish. Use honey to brush the grapes to be used for the decoration, sprinkle with the grated coconut, arrange around the pudding, and serve.

Practical Suggestions

To eliminate any air bubbles within the mold, do the following: fill it with the mixture, protect the mold with two folded terrycloth towels, strike it a number of times on the work surface, and then refrigerate. **See note on p. 73*

Apricot Ice Cream

INGREDIENTS
serves 4–6

3/4 lb. – 300 g APRICOTS
1 1/4 cups – 120 g SUGAR
2 cups MILK
A VANILLA bean
4 EGG YOLKS

For the garnish
1 oz. – 30 g CANDIED CITRON

EQUIPMENT
a saucepan
2 skillets
a blender
a mixing bowl
an electric ice cream machine
a serving bowl

Difficulty	AVERAGE
Preparation Time	20 MIN. + 20 MIN.
Cooking Time	30 MIN.
Method of cooking	STOVETOP
Microonde	NO
Freezing	YES
Keeping Time	3 DAYS

SPECIAL NOTE
Apricots were imported to the Mediterranean and Europe from the Orient by Alexander the Great and the Arabs. They were considered poisonous during the Middle Ages.

Recommended Wines
Gambellara Vin Santo (Veneto): liqueur–like wine or dry raisin wine served at 54°F / 12°C
Verdicchio di Matelica passito (Marche): liqueur–like wine or dry raisin wine served at 54°F / 12°C

1 Scald the apricots in a saucepan of boiling water, then drain, peel, pit and slice. Place in a skillet with a tablespoon of sugar and cook for 15 minutes over medium heat, stirring occasionally with a wooden spoon. Remove from the heat, set a tablespoon aside for the garnish and whip the rest in the blender.

2 Boil the milk in a skillet with the vanilla bean. Mix the egg yolks in a mixing bowl with the remaining sugar until you have a foamy mixture. Add the milk in a thin stream through a sieve, and mix. Remove the vanilla bean. Pour the mixture back into the skillet, place over moderate heat and bring almost to a boil, stirring constantly. As soon as it is thick enough to cover the spoon, remove it from the heat and cool, mixing occasionally to prevent the surface from hardening. Blend in the apricot whip, transfer everything to the ice cream machine, and set according to the instructions.

3 In the meantime, prepare the garnish. Cube the slices of apricot you set aside, and chop the citron into little leaf shapes. When the ice cream is ready, transfer it to the serving bowl and decorate with the cubes of apricot and leaves of candied citron.

Practical Suggestions
Apricots will keep in the refrigerator for a maximum of 7–10 days. To freeze or syrup them, use firm, solid fruit; to make jams, sorbets and ice cream, use ripe, sweet fruit.

Lemon Custard

Recommended Wines

Val d'Arbia Vin Santo (Tuscany): liqueur–like wine or dry raisin wine served at 54°F / 12°C

Carignano del Sulcis passito (Sardinia): liqueur–like wine or dry raisin wine served at 54°F / 12°C

1 Remove the zest of two lemons (only the yellow part), place a quart of water in a skillet and bring to a boil, and add the chopped butter and lemon zest.

2 Beat the egg yolks in a bowl with the sugar (set the whites aside). When the mixture is very foamy, add the sifted flour, and gradually dilute with the boiling water, butter and lemon zest mixture, stirring often.

3 Pour the mixture into a skillet, bring slowly to a boil and cook over very low heat for 10 minutes, mixing constantly. Remove the skillet from the heat, add the juice of three lemons, and gently fold in the egg whites, which you have beaten to peaks with a bit of salt in a separate mixing bowl. Pour the custard into a mold moistened with water, and refrigerate for about 3 hours.

4 In the meantime, prepare the garnish. In a small saucepan, bring about 1/3 cup – 1.5 dl water to boil with the sugar and cook about 3 minutes. Remove from the heat, add the sliced lemon and cool. Turn the custard mold out onto a serving dish, drain the lemon slices from the syrup, dry slightly, decorate the custard as you like, and serve.

Practical Suggestions

You should use organic lemons to prepare this custard. Serve with dry cookies such as ladyfingers.

INGREDIENTS

serves 6

3 LEMONS
1/4 cup – 40 g BUTTER
5 EGGS
1 1/2 cups – 150 g SUGAR
2/3 cup – 80 g WHITE FLOUR
1 pinch SALT

For the garnish

1 tablespoon SUGAR
one sliced LEMON

EQUIPMENT

a bowl, two skillets
a mixing bowl
a small saucepan
a mold
a serving dish

Difficulty	**AVERAGE**
Preparation Time	**20 MIN. + 3 HOURS**
Cooking Time	**20 MIN.**
Method of cooking	**STOVETOP**
Microonde	**NO**
Freezing	**NO**
Keeping Time	**2 DAYS**

SPECIAL NOTE

During Tabernacle celebrations, the Jews customarily carried a lemon in their left hand; it was considered a fragrant symbol to offer to God.

Fruit Salads and More

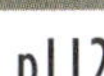

Fruit Compote

INGREDIENTS
serves 4–6

3 GREEN APPLES
juice of half a LEMON
12 oz. – 300 g APPLE JUICE
1 tablespoon GRATED ORANGE RIND
2 CINNAMON sticks
1/2 lb. – 200 g CALIFORNIA PRUNES
1/4 lb. – 100 g DRIED APRICOTS
2 oz. – 50 g WALNUT KERNELS

EQUIPMENT
a skillet
a mixing bowl
a serving bowl

Difficulty	**AVERAGE**
Preparation Time	**40 MIN.**
Cooking Time	**20–25 MIN.**
Method of cooking	**STOVETOP**
Microwave	**NO**
Freezing	**NO**
Keeping Time	**2 DAYS**

SPECIAL NOTE
Alcohol is extracted from plums to make various types of liquors. The sloe or blackthorn is used to make *slivovitz*, while Italian and French plum brandy is made from mature plums.

RECOMMENDED WINES

Moscato d'Asti (Piedmont): aged red wine served at 50°F / 10°C
Bianco di Scandiano Spumante (Emilia–Romagna): aged red wine served at 50°F / 10°C

1 Wash and dry the apples, peel, remove the core and slice thinly. Place in a mixing bowl and drizzle with the lemon juice to prevent them from browning. Place a cup of water in a skillet with the apple juice, grated orange rind and cinnamon sticks. Bring to a boil, then add the sliced apples, prunes and apricots.

2 Continue cooking for 12–14 minutes, stirring occasionally with a wooden spoon, until the sliced apples are cooked but still intact. Remove the mixture from the heat, let it cool, cover the skillet and refrigerate for at least an hour before serving.

3 A few minutes before serving, heat the walnut kernels in boiling water for a few minutes, remove the skin and place them in a hot oven to toast for a couple of minutes.

4 Remove the container form the refrigerator, discard the cinnamon sticks, place the skillet over moderate heat and gently heat the mixture. Transfer to a serving bowl, add the walnut kernels, mix gently, and serve hot or lukewarm.

PRACTICAL SUGGESTIONS

Fruit compote prepared in this manner is excellent for breakfast or for an afternoon tea. As dried fruit is very high in calories, it's better not to serve it as an after-meal dessert.

Candied Orange Peel

RECOMMENDED WINES

Alto Adige Moscato giallo (Trentino Alto Adige): liqueur–like wine or sweet raisin wine served at 50°F / 10°C

Oltrepò Pavese Moscato (Lombardy): aged red wine served at 50°F / 10°C

1 Remove the two ends of the orange, and using a small, very sharp knife, cut the remaining rind into 4 quarters, leaving a third of the pulp attached, and cut into strips about a half an inch – 1 centimeter wide.

2 Place the orange rind in a skillet and cover with cold water. Bring to a boil and drain, then repeat two more times, to remove the bitter taste and any impurities.

3 Place the drained rind back in the skillet, add a cup – a quarter liter of water and the sugar, stir, place the skillet on the heat and bring to a boil, stirring occasionally with a fork. Cook over moderate heat for about 30 minutes, until the rinds are shiny and transparent and the liquid has completely evaporated.

4 Place on a grill and arrange so they do not touch each other, and let them cool and dry completely. Dip them repeatedly in the sugar, arrange harmoniously on a serving dish and serve after dinner as an accompaniment to a good cognac or malt whiskey, or with pastries and tea.

PRACTICAL SUGGESTIONS

When you have to use citrus rinds for a recipe, as in this case, try to use organic fruit. In any case, before using them, be sure to wash them thoroughly under running water.

INGREDIENTS

serves 8

4 ORANGES with thick rind
2 1/4 cups – 200 g SUGAR

For the garnish

2 tablespoons SUGAR

EQUIPMENT

a skillet
a serving dish
or a tray

Difficulty	**AVERAGE**
Preparation Time	**10 MIN.**
Cooking Time	**50 MIN.**
Method of cooking	**STOVETOP**
Microwave	**NO**
Freezing	**NO**
Keeping Time	**3 DAYS**

SPECIAL NOTE

There are many varieties of oranges. Those with red flesh are known as blood oranges, while lighter colored ones are known as navel or Valencia oranges.

Sour Cherry Soup

INGREDIENTS

serves 4

2 lb. – 800 g SOUR CHERRIES
1 1/4 cup – 5 dl RED WINE
4 tablespoons SUGAR
small piece of CINNAMON stick
half a LEMON zest
1/2 lb. – 200 g SPONGE CAKE

EQUIPMENT

a skillet
plastic wrap
4 glass serving cups

Difficulty	AVERAGE
Preparation Time	15 MIN.
Cooking Time	10 MIN.
Method of cooking	STOVETOP
Microwave	NO
Freezing	NO
Keeping Time	1 DAY

SPECIAL NOTE

Sour cherries, also known as morello cherries, ripen between July and August, later than other types of cherries. Some of the most popular varieties are the Piedmont morello and the Zara sour cherry.

Recommended Wines

Moscato Passito di Pantelleria (Sicily): liqueur–like wine or dry raisin wine served at 50°F / 10°C

Moscato d'Asti (Piedmont): aged red wine served at 50°F / 10°C

1 Remove the cherry stems, and wash and pit the cherries. Place over the heat in a skillet with the wine, sugar and cinnamon and the yellow part of the lemon zest, sliced thinly.

2 Cover the container and cook over low heat, calculating 10 minutes from when it begins to boil. Then let the cherries sit in the cooking liquid.

3 In the meantime, cut the sponge cake into thin slices and place in the bottom of each individual cup. Remove the cinnamon from the cherries and pour them over the sponge cake with the liquid.

4 Let the preparation cool, cover the cups with plastic wrap and refrigerate for a few hours before serving.

Practical Suggestions

For a more flavorful dish, add a few tablespoons English cream on the slices of sponge cake, or garnish with dabs of whipped cream.

Apple Fritters with Macaroons

INGREDIENTS
serves 4

4 MACAROONS
1 1/2 cups – 180 g WHITE FLOUR
1 tablespoon BAKING POWDER
2 EGGS
3/4 cup – 80 g SUGAR
1 pinch CINNAMON
2 tablespoons MARSALA WINE
1/2 cup – 2 dl MILK
4 APPLES
PEANUT oil for frying
1 tablespoon POWDERED SUGAR

EQUIPMENT
a mixing bowl, an apple corer
a frying pan
or a fryer
absorbent paper towels
a serving dish

Difficulty	EASY
Preparation Time	20 MIN. + 3 HOURS
Cooking Time	10 MIN.
Method of cooking	STOVETOP
Microwave	NO
Freezing	NO
Keeping Time	1 DAY

SPECIAL NOTE
Eating an apple will remove food residue from between the teeth, keeps the gum tissue healthy and stimulates the production of saliva.

RECOMMENDED WINES

Asti Spumante (Piedmont): dry sparkling wine served at 46°F / 8°C
Colli di Parma Malvasia Spumante (Emilia–Romagna): dry sparkling wine served at 46°F / 8°C

1 Crumble the macaroons coarsely and mix the flour with the baking powder. Beat the eggs in a mixing bowl with the sugar, then add the macaroons, flour, cinnamon, Marsala and milk, and mix well with a wooden spoon. Cover the batter and let it sit about 3 hours.

2 Wash the apples, remove the core and cut them horizontally into slices about a half an inch – one centimeter thick. Heat a generous amount of oil in a frying pan or fryer, and as soon as it is hot, dip the apples in the batter and fry them to golden brown.

3 Let the slices brown for a few minutes, remove with a slotted spatula, and place on paper towels to absorb any excess oil. Transfer to a serving dish, sprinkle with the powdered sugar and serve immediately.

PRACTICAL SUGGESTIONS

These are the most characteristic and traditional fritters in Italian cooking, especially as a children's snack around Carnival (Mardi Gras) time. You can serve them with fritole (fritters with raisins and pine nuts) or even banana or pear fritters similar to these (just change the fruit). If you want, you can add a handful of softened, dried raisins to the batter.

Strawberries with Red Wine

INGREDIENTS

serves 4

1 1/2 lb. – 600 g ALPINE STRAWBERRIES
2 cups – half a liter SWEET RED WINE
4 tablespoons SUGAR
half a CINNAMON stick
1 LEMON zest
3 MINT leaves

EQUIPMENT

absorbent paper towels
a bowl
a serving cup

Difficulty	EASY
Preparation Time	10 MIN. + 1 HOUR
Cooking Time	NO
Method of cooking	NO
Microwave	NO
Freezing	NO
Keeping Time	1 DAY

SPECIAL NOTE

Mint is the aromatic herb par excellence in Mongolian cooking, and is widely used in India and the Middle East as well. It maintains its flavor and fragrance even when dried.

Recommended Wines

Colli dell'Etruria Centrale Vin Santo (Tuscany): Liqueur–like wine or dry raisin wine served at 50°F / 10°C

Brachetto d'Acqui (Piedmont): aged red wine served at 54°F / 12°C

1 Quickly wash the alpine strawberries in ice water, then dry on absorbent paper towels and remove the stems.

2 Transfer to a bowl, add the wine, mix gently with a wooden spoon and let the bowl sit in a cool place for an hour, mixing occasionally so the wine blends in completely.

3 When ready to serve, transfer the strawberries to the serving bowl, and sprinkle the surface with a few pieces of cinnamon, strips of lemon zest and fresh mint leaves.

Practical Suggestions

Alpine strawberries are available year round. Because they are quite perishable, you should use them quickly and try to handle them as little as possible. The original recipe calls for a wine called fragolino, *obtained from so-called "strawberry" grapes or American grapes.*

Pears with Barolo

INGREDIENTS

serves 6

4 PEARS with firm flesh
4 tablespoons SUGAR
1 stick CINNAMON
3 CLOVES
3 cups – 3/4 liter BAROLO WINE

EQUIPMENT

a baking dish
a small saucepan
a serving bowl

Difficulty	AVERAGE
Preparation Time	10 MIN.
Cooking Time	1 HOUR
Method of cooking	OVEN
Microwave	NO
Freezing	NO
Keeping Time	3 DAYS

SPECIAL NOTE

Barolo is a red Piedmont wine produced with Nebbiolo grapes. It can be sold only after being aged for three years, two of which are in oak and chestnut barrels.

Recommended Wines

Barolo (Piedmont): full-bodied red wine served at 68°F / 20°C
Valtellina Superiore (Lombardy): full-bodied red wine served at 68°F / 20°C

1 Carefully wash the pears, dry well with a dishtowel, place in a baking dish, if possible with tall sides, and sprinkle with the sugar.

2 Place the cinnamon stick and cloves with the pears, and pour on the Barolo so it covers them almost completely. Bake in a preheated 350°oven about an hour.

3 When done, remove from the oven, discard the cinnamon and the cloves, and transfer to a serving bowl or individual serving cups if you wish, then drizzle with their cooking liquid. Let them cool 30 minutes and serve.

Practical Suggestions

If the pears' cooking liquid is too thin, place it in a small saucepan and reduce it over high heat, then pour it over the fruit. You should use firm-fleshed pears for this recipe, such as Martin Sec from Valle d'Aosta. For an impressive presentation, cut the half pears with the skin facing upward, keeping them connected by the stem portion, and open them up like fans.

Stuffed Peaches

INGREDIENTS

serves 4

24 SHELLED ALMONDS
4 PEACHES
1 EGG
2 tablespoons SUGAR
1/4 lb. – 100 g CANDIED FRUIT
1/2 cup – 2 dl FORTIFIED WINE (or liqueur)

EQUIPMENT

a mortar
a skillet
a mixing bowl
a baking dish
a serving dish

Difficulty	**EASY**
Preparation Time	**10 MIN.**
Cooking Time	**25 MIN.**
Method of cooking	**OVEN**
Microwave	**NO**
Freezing	**NO**
Keeping Time	**1 DAY**

SPECIAL NOTE

Peaches are members of the Rosaceae family, and probably originated in China. They spread to other areas of Asia in the remote past and were introduced to Europe in Roman times.

RECOMMENDED WINES

Cinque Terre Sciacchetrà (Liguria): liqueur–like wine or dry raisin wine served at 50°F / 10°C

Gambellara Recioto (Veneto): liqueur–like wine or dry raisin wine served at 50°F / 10°C

❖

1 Toast the almonds for a few minutes in a hot oven. Remove, and as soon as they are cold, rub them between your hands to remove the skin. Crush them in the mortar and then transfer them to a mixing bowl.

2 Place a generous amount of water in a skillet, and when it comes to a boil, immerse the peaches for a minute. Drain, peel, cut in two and remove the pit, then take a bit of the pulp from each one and mince finely.

3 Add the egg, sugar, minced peach pulp and chopped candied fruit to the almonds, then mix well and fill the peach halves with the mixture.

4 Lightly butter the baking dish, arrange the stuffed peaches on it, drizzle with the wine and bake in a preheated 320°F oven for about 20 minutes.

5 When done, remove the peaches and transfer to a serving dish. If you like, decorate with mint leaves, then let them cool before serving.

PRACTICAL SUGGESTIONS

If you want, you can garnish the peaches with a dab of whipped cream or a scoop of vanilla or custard ice cream. Cooking time for this recipe may vary depending on the ripeness and variety of the peaches.

Fruit Salad in Pineapple Bowl

INGREDIENTS

serves 4

2 small PINEAPPLES
1 ORANGE
2 MANDARIN ORANGES
1 BANANA
1 KIWI
SUGAR as necessary
juice of 1 LEMON
VANILLA ICE CREAM as necessary

EQUIPMENT

a mixing bowl
plastic wrap
4 individual plates

Difficulty	AVERAGE
Preparation Time	30'
Cooking Time	NO
Method of cooking	NO
Microwave	NO
Freezing	NO
Keeping Time	1 DAY

SPECIAL NOTE

Unlike other citrus fruits, mandarin oranges spread to the West only in the early 19th century, as an ornamental plant. Cultivation for food purposes began 50 years later in Algeria and Sicily.

RECOMMENDED WINES

Moscato Passito di Pantelleria (Sicily): liqueur–like wine or dry raisin wine served at 50°F / 10°C
Collio Goriziano Picolit (Friuli–Venezia Giulia): liqueur–like wine or dry raisin wine served at 50°F / 10°C

1 Wash the pineapples and chop in half lengthwise, being careful not to remove the crown. Using a small, sharp knife, cut out the pineapple and place the skins in the refrigerator.

2 Chop the pineapple into cubes, peel the orange and mandarins down to the pulp, removing the seeds and skin between the segments, peel the banana and chop into rounds, and peel and chop the kiwi.

3 Place all the fruit into a mixing bowl, sprinkle with sugar and lemon juice and mix rapidly. Cover with plastic wrap and refrigerate until ready to serve.

4 Remove the pineapple skin from the refrigerator, transfer to individual plates, place the fruit salad in each of them, place a scoop of ice cream in the center, and serve immediately.

PRACTICAL SUGGESTIONS

To peel orange and mandarin segments to the pulp without ruining them, use scissors to cut the skin along the edge, open it and remove the flesh. Don't discard citrus rinds; a few pieces thrown onto the gas flame will help eliminate kitchen odors.

Stewed Apricots

Recommended Wines

Marsala dolce (Sicily): aged red wine served at 50°F / 10°C
Verdicchio di Matelica passito (Marche): liqueur–like wine or dry raisin wine served at 50°F / 10°C

1 Wash the apricots well under running water, cut in half, remove the pit and dry on absorbent paper towels.

2 Melt the butter in a saucepan over low heat and add the apricots, with the cut side down. Sprinkle with sugar, drizzle with marsala and cook over very low heat for 25–30 minutes.

3 When done (they should be firm and not falling apart), remove the pan from the heat and transfer the apricots to a serving dish, drizzle with cooking liquid, cool and serve.

Practical Suggestions

The apricots will be just as tasty if you use a small amount of sherry instead of the marsala. In both cases, if you think the amount of liquor indicated will give the dish too strong a flavor, you can reduce the quantity to just one small glass diluted with a glass of water.

INGREDIENTS

serves 4

8 rather large APRICOTS
2 tablespoons – 20 g BUTTER
1 1/8 cup – 100 g SUGAR
2 small glasses SWEET MARSALA WINE

EQUIPMENT

a saucepan
absorbent paper towels
a serving dish

Difficulty	**EASY**
Preparation Time	**10 MIN.**
Cooking Time	**30 MIN.**
Method of cooking	**STOVETOP**
Microwave	**NO**
Freezing	**NO**
Keeping Time	**3 DAYS**

SPECIAL NOTE

There are two main varieties of marsala wine: dry and sweet. Brillat-Savarin suggested serving a small glass (dry, of course) after a consommé.

Stuffed Pink Grapefruit Cups

INGREDIENTS

serves 6

3 PINK GRAPEFRUITS
1 PINEAPPLE
1 MANGO
6 PEACHES
several large GREEN and PURPLE GRAPES
3 tablespoons RAW CANE SUGAR
2 tablespoons LEMON JUICE
1 container RASPBERRIES
3 tablespoons POMEGRANATE SYRUP
a few FRESH MINT leaves

EQUIPMENT

a glass bowl
chipped glass
plastic wrap
6 glass serving cups

Difficulty	AVERAGE
Preparation Time	35 MIN. + 3 HOURS
Cooking Time	NO
Method of cooking	NO
Microwave	NO
Freezing	NO
Keeping Time	1 DAY

SPECIAL NOTE

According to ancient legend, the Indian god Shiva created the majestic mango tree as a gift to his wife Parvati. India is the number one mango producer and exporter in the world.

Recommended Wines

Vignanello Greco Spumante (Lazio): aged red wine served at 46°F / 8°C
Moscato di Trani dolce naturale (Puglia): aged red wine served at 50°F / 10°C

1 Cut the grapefruits horizontally in half, and using a small knife, gently remove the pulp, keeping the skins intact and placing them in the refrigerator. Peel the pulp down to the flesh, remove the seeds, cut into cubes and place in a bowl. Remove the pineapple skin and the hard central part, and chop the pineapple into cubes.

2 Add the cubed pineapple, the peeled, chopped mango with the seed removed, the peeled, pitted and chopped peaches, and the grapes (thrown into boiling water for a few moments and then peeled) to the grapefruit pulp.

3 Sprinkle everything with sugar, drizzle with lemon juice, mix gently with a wooden spoon, cover with plastic wrap and refrigerate for 3 hours, adding the raspberries at the last moment.

4 When ready to serve, place a base of chopped ice mixed with the pomegranate syrup in each serving cup, for a pretty pink color. Fill the grapefruit halves with the fruit salad, garnish with mint, place on the ice and serve.

Practical Suggestions

To clean the mango, cut it lengthwise down to the seed, and slip the knife between the pulp and seed to separate them. Cut the pulp inside the skin with a sharp knife, first in one direction and then another, to obtain cubes that you can push out by pressing on the skin side. At this point it will be easy to remove them with a knife.

Busecchina

INGREDIENTS
serves 4

1 lb. – 450 g DRIED CHESTNUTS
1 teaspoon VANILLA
2 cups – half a liter SWEET WHITE WINE

For the garnish
1 cup – 1/4 liter WHIPPING CREAM

EQUIPMENT
2 mixing bowls
1 toothbrush with stiff bristles
a pot
a pastry syringe
4 individual serving cups

Difficulty	EASY
Preparation Time	20 MIN. + 12 HOURS
Cooking Time	3 HOURS
Method of cooking	STOVETOP
Microwave	NO
Freezing	NO
Keeping Time	1 DAY

SPECIAL NOTE
The famous Etna chestnut tree is known as the "chestnut of the hundred horses," because it once protected Queen Giovanna and her entire entourage under its branches during a storm.

RECOMMENDED WINES
Oltrepò Pavese Moscato (Lombardy): aged red wine served at 46°F / 8°C
Freisa di Chieri sweet (Piedmont): aged red wine served at 45°F / 12°C

1 The evening before you prepare the dish, rinse the dry chestnuts, place in a mixing bowl and cover with tepid water, then soak till the next morning. Drain, and use the toothbrush to remove the skins.

2 Place the chestnuts in a large pot, cover with water, add the vanilla and cook about 3 hours (adding wine near the end of cooking) over very low heat to prevent them from breaking. When done, they should have absorbed all the liquid.

3 In the meantime, beat the cream to peaks in a mixing bowl. When the chestnuts are ready, place them in the individual serving cups while still lukewarm, place the whipped cream in the pastry syringe, decorate the chestnuts, and serve.

PRACTICAL SUGGESTIONS
Busecchina is a very simple, economical dessert from Lombardy that is nevertheless quite nutritious and tasty. It's also excellent as a children's snack. If you want to make the dessert more flavorful, add a small glass of amaretto liqueur instead of the wine, a few minutes before you remove the chestnuts from the heat.

Pears with Chocolate

INGREDIENTS

serves 4

4 PEARS
3 tablespoons HONEY
1/4 lb. – 100 g DARK CHOCOLATE
1 oz. – 20 g BUTTER
1 EGG

EQUIPMENT

a skillet
2 small saucepans
a mixing bowl
a serving dish

Difficulty	AVERAGE
Preparation Time	20 MIN.
Cooking Time	40 MIN.
Method of cooking	STOVETOP
Microwave	NO
Freezing	NO
Keeping Time	2 DAYS

SPECIAL NOTE

Pears contain a small amount of sugars, which are absorbed rapidly by the body and supply quick energy. They are therefore ideal for light snacks.

RECOMMENDED WINES

Brachetto d'Acqui (Piedmont): aged red wine served at 57°F / 14°C
Trentino Vin Santo (Trentino Alto Adige): liqueur–like wine or dry raisin wine served at 50°F / 10°C

1 Wash the pears well, peel them, leaving them whole and with the stem. Place in a skillet in which you have added a glass of water, and let them cook over low heat, covered, for about a half hour, or until they are almost done. Drain and arrange on a serving dish.

2 Dissolve the honey with 4 tablespoons hot water in a small saucepan, and pour it over the pears. Cool. In the meantime, flake the chocolate, place over the heat in another small saucepan with 3–4 tablespoons water, and melt.

3 Remove the small saucepan from the heat, and cool the chocolate to lukewarm. Add the butter, chopped, and the egg yolk. Mix well to blend the ingredients.

4 In a mixing bowl, beat the egg white to stiff peaks and fold gently into the mixture. When ready, pour over the cooled pears and serve.

PRACTICAL SUGGESTIONS

You can flavor the chocolate cream with two teaspoons pear concentrate. A variation of this recipe is to cook the pears in a syrup prepared with 1 1/8 cup – 100 g sugar, 2/3 cup – 3 dl water, half a vanilla bean, the zest and juice of one lemon, and a teaspoon of pear grappa. Sieve the cooking liquid and place in a serving dish before adding the cooked pears to it.

Flambéed Bananas

INGREDIENTS

serves 4

1 LEMON
1 ORANGE
1/4 cup – 50 g BUTTER
1 1/3 cup – 125 g REFINED SUGAR
RUM to taste
1 teaspoon VANILLA
5 tablespoons – 50 g CREAM
6 SUGAR cubes
4 BANANAS

EQUIPMENT

a silver–plated frying pan
or tin–plated copper frying pan

Difficulty	AVERAGE
Preparation Time	15 MIN.
Cooking Time	5 MIN
Method of cooking	STOVETOP
Microwave	YES
Freezing	NO
Keeping Time	1 DAY

SPECIAL NOTE

Bananas for export are harvested green and kept at around 55°F even during transport on special ships. They are then ripened artificially.

RECOMMENDED WINES

Primitivo di Manduria Liquoroso dolce naturale (Puglia): liqueur–like wine or dry raisin wine served at 54°F / 12°C
Moscato Passito di Pantelleria (Sicily): liqueur–like wine or dry raisin wine served at 54°F / 12°C

1 Wash and thoroughly dry the lemon and orange. Using a small, well-sharpened knife, peel them, if possible in a spiral to keep the peel in one piece. Peel the bananas, cut in half width–wise, then in half lengthwise.

2 Melt the butter in a frying pan over moderate heat, then remove from the heat. Add the refined sugar, two tablespoons rum, the vanilla, the cream and the citrus peels. Mix well with a wooden spoon to dissolve the sugar, then add the banana pieces, delicately turning a few times until they are well seasoned. Place the pan back on the flame, lower the heat and cook about 3 minutes.

3 In the meantime, soak the sugar cubes in rum, and after waiting one minute, place them at a distance from one another in the frying pan. Flambé the sugar cubes and serve while still lit.

PRACTICAL SUGGESTIONS

This recipe requires you to cook and flambé while your guests watch, but if you don't have a gas burner or spirit stove and a silver-plated or tin-plated copper pan, you can prepare the already cooked bananas in the kitchen, on a heated serving dish, sprinkle them with rum and flambé. If you're careful, they'll still be flaming when you get them to the table.

Apricots with Apricot Brandy

INGREDIENTS

serves 6

18 APRICOTS
4 tablespoons SUGAR
SUGAR to taste
half a cup APRICOT BRANDY
3/4 lb. – 300 g CUSTARD ICE CREAM
1/2 lb. – 220 g SLIVERED ALMONDS
3/4 lb. – 300 g APRICOT ICE CREAM

EQUIPMENT

absorbent kitchen towels
a skillet
6 individual serving cups

Difficulty	EASY
Preparation Time	15 MIN.
Cooking Time	10 MIN.
Method of cooking	STOVETOP
Microwave	NO
Freezing	YES
Keeping Time	1 DAY

SPECIAL NOTE

Apricot brandy is a wine distillate flavored with apricots. It is common in all countries that produce brandy, and is often used in baking.

Recommended Wines

Alghero Passito (Sardinia): liqueur–like wine or dry raisin wine served at 54°F / 12°C

Campi Flegrei Piedirosso (Campania): aged red wine served at 54°F / 12°C

1 Carefully wash the apricots, dry on absorbent kitchen towels, cut in half, remove the pit, and using a small sharp knife, cut into large wedges.

2 Place the wedges in a skillet, add the sugar and apricot brandy, and cook over high heat for 10 minutes. Then remove from the heat and cool the apricots completely.

3 Place a layer of custard ice cream in each serving cup, cover with a few apricots, sprinkle with the almonds, and add a layer of apricot ice cream. End with more apricots, garnish with slivered almonds, and serve immediately.

Practical Suggestions

To prepare this delicious dessert, you can use chopped hazelnuts instead of almonds, or else grated coconut. Any custard ice cream, such as French Vanilla, etc., will suffice.

0.25

Peaches in Maple Syrup

INGREDIENTS
serves 4

2 lb. – 800 g PEACHES
4 tablespoons MAPLE SYRUP

EQUIPMENT
a pot
a mixing bowl

Difficulty	EASY
Preparation Time	30 MIN. + 4 HOURS
Cooking Time	NO
Method of cooking	STOVETOP
Microwave	NO
Freezing	NO
Keeping Time	3 DAYS

SPECIAL NOTE

Maple syrup is quite popular in North American and Chinese cuisine, where it is used to flavor stews and to top pancakes and other sweets.

Recommended Wines

Colli di Parma Malvasia Spumante (Emilia-Romagna): aged red wine served at 50°F/10°C

Moscato d'Asti (Piedmont): aged red wine served at 46°F/8°C

❖

1 Wash the peaches and immerse in a pot with a generous amount of boiling water for a few minutes. Remove with a slotted spoon, peel quickly and cut in two, removing the seed.

2 Place the hot peach halves in a mixing bowl, sprinkle with maple syrup and cover the mixing bowl with a cover, so the heat disperses slowly. The heat will help the peaches absorb more of the syrup.

3 Leave the peaches in the mixing bowl for about an hour, covered. After they reach room temperature, refrigerate 3 hours before serving.

Practical Suggestions

If you don't have maple syrup, this dessert will be just as good if you use corn syrup or honey. You can accompany it with vanilla cream served in a sauce boat.

Pears with Cheese

Recommended Wines

Colli Orientali del Friuli Ramandolo (Friuli Venezia Giulia): aged red wine served at 54°F / 12°C

Elba Vin Santo (Tuscany): liqueur.like wine or dry raisin wine served at 54°F / 12°C

1 Wash the pears and peel them, leaving the stems on. Pour 1/2 cup – 2 dl water, the cider and the honey in a saucepan and bring to a boil. Boil about 20 minutes, then add the pears and cook over moderate heat for about 10 minutes, turning from time to time.

2 In the meantime, prepare the cheese cream. Cut the roquefort into pieces and sieve it, then place in a mixing bowl. Add the mascarpone and mix with a wooden spoon until you have a smooth, uniform cream.

3 When the pears are ready, use a slotted spoon to remove them from the saucepan and cool them completely. Dry with a very clean cloth or absorbent paper towels and cut in half. Core them and enlarge the cavity a bit. Transfer to a serving dish.

4 Pour the cheese cream into a pastry bag with a fluted tip and squeeze the cream in the pear cavities, filling generously. Serve the pears with the cheese cream at room temperature.

Practical Suggestions

Kaiser pears are the best for this recipe. To peel them uniformly without removing too much pulp, use a potato peeler. To ensure that they are well-cooked, just prick them with a toothpick.

INGREDIENTS

serves 4

2 PEARS
1/2 cup – 2 dl PEAR or apple cider
2 oz. – 50 g HONEY
1/3 lb. – 150 g ROQUEFORT CHEESE
1/4 lb. – 80 g MASCARPONE

EQUIPMENT

a saucepan
a mixing bowl
a corer
a pastry bag with fluted tip
a serving dish

Difficulty	**AVERAGE**
Preparation Time	**15 MIN.**
Cooking Time	**30 MIN.**
Method of cooking	**STOVETOP**
Microwave	**NO**
Freezing	**NO**
Keeping Time	**1 DAY**

SPECIAL NOTE

Mascarpone is a fat, creamy cheese made from the cream of cow's milk, processed and coagulated through acidification using citric or tartaric acid and milk enzymes.

Crêpes with Apples and Apricots

INGREDIENTS

serves 4

1/8 cup – 30 g BUTTER
3 APPLES, peeled and chopped into cubes
3 APRICOTS, sliced
1/2 cup – 60 g SUGAR
1.5 oz. – 30 g SLIVERED ALMONDS
8 CRÊPES, already made

For the cream

1/8 cup – 30 g BUTTER
2 oz. – 50 g POWDERED SUGAR
3 oz. – 70 g ALMONDS, peeled and ground
1 tablespoon RUM

EQUIPMENT

a cast iron frying pan
a small saucepan
a bowl, a baking dish

Difficulty	**AVERAGE**
Preparation Time	**15 MIN.**
Cooking Time	**30 MIN.**
Method of cooking	**STOVETOP AND OVEN**
Microwave	**YES**
Freezing	**YES**
Keeping Time	**2 DAYS**

SPECIAL NOTE

Simple and popular, over the past few decades crêpes have become the basis for improvised snacks as well as dishes served in fine restaurants.

RECOMMENDED WINES

Montecarlo Vin Santo (Tuscany): aged red wine served at 54°F / 12°C
Recioto di Soave (Veneto): liqueur–like wine or dry raisin wine served at 50°F / 10°C

1 Place 2/3 – 20 g of the butter, and the apples, in the cast iron pan, sauté briefly and add the apricots, and continue cooking for 5 minutes, mixing often with a wooden spoon. When half done, add the sugar and mix from time to time until the apples become a nice golden brown. Then add the almonds and blend, mixing gently.

2 Place the crêpes on a work surface, place a bit of the mixture in the center of each one, and roll it up into a tube.

3 Prepare the cream. Soften the butter to room temperature, place it in a bowl and beat until it is fluffy and foamy. Add the sugar and the almonds a little at a time, mix until you have a uniform mixture, and add the rum at the end.

4 Place the crêpes in a lightly buttered baking dish and spread a thin layer of the cream over them. Bake in a preheated 400°F oven for 8–10 minutes, until the crêpes are browned. Remove and serve hot or lukewarm in the baking dish.

PRACTICAL SUGGESTIONS

If you serve this dessert hot, you can lightly sprinkle the crêpes with rum or brandy and flambé them as you bring them to the table. Canned apricots in syrup can be used instead of fresh ones. Be sure to drain them.

Fig Fritters

INGREDIENTS

makes 20 fritters

1 1/4 cup – 150 g WHITE FLOUR
1 tablespoon SESAME OIL
2.5 oz. – 60 g SKINNED and TOASTED ALMONDS
1 oz. – 20 g PINE NUTS
1 oz. – 25 g RAISINS
half a small glass RUM
1 pinch POWDERED CINNAMON
1 pinch POWDERED CLOVES
20 DRIED FIGS
SUNFLOWER SEED oil for frying

EQUIPMENT

a mixing bowl, a small bowl
a frying pan
absorbent paper towels
a serving dish

Difficulty	**EASY**
Preparation Time	**1 HOUR + 10 MIN.**
Cooking Time	**10 MIN.**
Method of cooking	**STOVETOP**
Microwave	**NO**
Freezing	**NO**
Keeping Time	**2–3 DAYS**

SPECIAL NOTE

Figs have been a food staple for people and armies since ancient times. The Roman legions fed on bread, olives, sheep's cheese and figs.

RECOMMENDED WINES

Verdicchio dei Castelli di Jesi passito (Marche): liqueur–like wine or dry raisin wine served at 54°F / 12°C
Moscato di Trani dolce naturale (Puglia): aged red wine served at 54°F / 12°C

1 Dissolve the flour a little at a time with a few tablespoons water in a mixing bowl. Add a tablespoon sesame oil to make a creamy, soft batter.

2 Coarsely chop the almonds and pine nuts. Chop the raisins in two, remove the seeds and soften them for half an hour in a small bowl with the rum. Place these ingredients, including the rum, in a mixing bowl, and make a uniform mixture. Add the cinnamon and cloves and mix again well.

3 Using a small sharp knife, cut open the figs like a book, leaving them joined by one side, and fill them with small amounts of the mixture. Press around the cut to close them well, and shape the fig back into its original form.

4 Heat a generous amount of oil in a frying pan, dip the figs one by one in the batter and fry them to a uniform golden brown in the hot oil. When ready, remove them with a slotted spatula, place on absorbent paper towels and then on a serving dish, and serve immediately.

PRACTICAL SUGGESTIONS

The dry figs and the batter are sweet enough to make the addition of any sugar inadvisable. If you want, after they're fried you can sprinkle them with a bit of vanilla-flavored sugar. The fritters can also be served as a children's snack or as an accompaniment to tea.

Candied Chocolate Oranges

INGREDIENTS

serves 4

2.2 lb. – 1 kg ORANGES
SUGAR as necessary
1/4 lb. – 100 g BAR DARK CHOCOLATE

EQUIPMENT

a bowl
a small saucepan
fluted paper muffin cups
a serving dish

Difficulty	AVERAGE
Preparation Time	30 MIN. + 3 DAYS
Cooking Time	20 MIN.
Method of cooking	STOVETOP
Microwave	NO
Freezing	NO
Keeping Time	7 DAYS

SPECIAL NOTE

Oranges stimulate the digestion, calm the nervous system and act as an expectorant. In China, both immature and fully ripe oranges are used for medicinal purposes.

RECOMMENDED WINES

Greco di Bianco (Calabria): aged red wine served at 50°F / 10°C
Malvasia delle Lipari passito (Sicily): liqueur–like wine or dry raisin wine served at 54°F / 12°C

1 Wash the oranges well, and using a small sharp knife, remove the orange part of the rind. Cut it into little strips, which you should set in a bowl under running water for 12 hours. Then drain them, mince, weigh, and place in a small saucepan with an equal amount of sugar.

2 Cook for 5–6 minutes, remove from the heat, and repeat the cooking process, without adding anything else, once a day for 3 consecutive days. In the end, you should have a dry mixture. When the cooking procedure is completed, grate the bar of chocolate into flakes.

3 Make little walnut size balls from the candied orange paste, then roll them in the flaked chocolate, pressing lightly. Place in the paper muffin cups and arrange on a serving dish.

PRACTICAL SUGGESTIONS

As this recipe uses only the orange rind, you should try to find organic oranges. You can serve these sweets as an unusual dessert or an accompaniment to tea in place of cookies.

Stuffed Prunes

INGREDIENTS

serves 4

20 PITTED PRUNES
2 tablespoons RUM
20 SHELLED ALMONDS
1/4 lb. – 100 g DARK CHOCOLATE

EQUIPMENT

a mixing bowl
absorbent paper towels
a serving dish

Difficulty	AVERAGE
Preparation Time	20 MIN. + 20 MIN.
Cooking Time	NO
Method of cooking	NO
Microwave	NO
Freezing	NO
Keeping Time	5 DAYS

SPECIAL NOTE

There are many varieties of plums that can be dried to make prunes. Some of these include the Agen, the Stanley, and the Italian plum. California also produces excellent prunes.

RECOMMENDED WINES

Recioto di Soave (Veneto): liqueur–like wine or dry raisin wine served at 54°F / 12°C

Cesanese di Affile dolce (Lazio): aged red wine served at 50°F / 10°C

❖

1 Place the prunes in a mixing bowl and drizzle with the rum. Then pour enough lukewarm water over them to cover completely, and soak about 20 minutes.

2 In the meantime, immerse the almonds in boiling water, drain after a few minutes, peel and dry. Grate the chocolate. When the prunes have plumped, drain and dry with absorbent paper towels.

3 Cut open the prunes, stuff with a bit of chocolate, place an almond in the center and arrange on a serving dish. Serve decorated with flakes of chocolate.

PRACTICAL SUGGESTIONS

For this recipe to be successful, you need large, excellent quality prunes that are quite fleshy. For a richer stuffing, mix the grated chocolate with 2 oz. ricotta and use the resulting mixture to fill the prunes. You can use halved walnut kernels instead of almonds, and if you want, you can also stuff with a bit of your favorite jam.

Nuoro Orange Juice

INGREDIENTS
serves 4

1/4 lb. – 100 g ORANGE PEEL
(only the orange portion)
1/4 lb. – 100 g SHELLED ALMONDS
1/4 lb. – 100 g HONEY

EQUIPMENT
a glass mixing bowl
a skillet
a marble surface or baking sheet
a serving dish

Difficulty	AVERAGE
Preparation Time	30 MIN. + 48 HOURS
Cooking Time	40 HOURS
Method of cooking	STOVETOP AND OVEN
Microwave	NO
Freezing	NO
Keeping Time	3 DAYS

SPECIAL NOTE
The highest quality, most common type of blood orange is the Tarocco. It is bright red, seedless and has a thin skin. The Sanguinella is another later variety.

Recommended Wines
Malvasia di Bosa (Sardinia): aged red wine served at 54°F / 12°C
Nasco di Cagaliari dolce (Sardinia): aged red wine served at 50°F / 10°C

1 Cut the orange peel into little strips a little over an inch long and about a quarter inch wide (3 centimeters long and half a centimeter wide). Place in a glass mixing bowl, cover with water and soak for two days, changing the water occasionally, so it loses its bitter taste. Then drain well and dry.

2 Immerse the almonds in boiling water for a few minutes, drain, skin, dry and toast for about 10 minutes in a 320°F–340°F oven, then sliver.

3 Place the orange rind and honey in a skillet over low heat, and cook 25–30 minutes, stirring continuously with a wooden spoon. Add the almonds, mix well and remove from the heat.

4 Spread the mixture on a marble surface or a baking sheet, smooth with the blade of a knife dipped in water, and when it is cooled to lukewarm but still soft, cut into pieces. Cool, transfer to a serving dish and serve.

Practical Suggestions
The mixture has to be spread as uniformly as possible for this recipe to be successful. For best results, after you pour it out onto a marble surface or baking sheet, you should level it first with the moistened blade of a knife or a spatula, and then press it with a half an orange or lemon.